Communities and Sustainable Forestry in Developing Countries

A publication of the International Center for
Self-Governance

The mission of the International Center for Self-Governance is to encourage men and women in developing countries to achieve self-governing and entrepreneurial ways of life. In addition to publishing the finest academic studies, such as this edition of *Communities and Sustainable Forestry in Developing Countries,* ICSG also provides practical materials in a variety of readily accessible formats, including manuals, learning tools, and interactive tasks.

Also available from ICSG is *Sustainable Community Forestry,* a companion video to this volume that highlights a self-governing forestry project. Shot in Nepal's Dhading district, *Sustainable Community Forestry* shows how a village user group is successfully managing a forest that had nearly been destroyed by overuse.

For more information on ICSG or its publications, training materials, and videos, please contact:

ICSG
720 Market Street
San Francisco, CA 94102 USA
(415) 981-5353

COMMUNITIES AND SUSTAINABLE FORESTRY IN DEVELOPING COUNTRIES

William Ascher

ICS PRESS

Institute for Contemporary Studies

San Francisco, California

This book is a publication of the International Center for Self-Governance, dedicated to promoting self-governing and entrepreneurial ways of life around the world. The Center is affiliated with the Institute for Contemporary Studies, a nonpartisan, nonprofit, public policy research organization. The analyses, conclusions, and opinions expressed in ICS Press publications are those of the authors and not necessarily those of the Institute for Contemporary Studies, or of its officers, its directors, or others associated with, or funding, its work.

Publication of this book was funded by the U.S. Agency for International Development. Research for the work was funded by ICSG and the Center for Tropical Conservation, each through cooperative agreements with USAID.

Inquiries, book orders, and catalog requests should be addressed to ICS Press, 720 Market Street, San Francisco, CA 94102 USA. Telephone: (415) 981-5353. Fax: (415) 986-4878. To order call toll free: (800) 326-0263.

98 97 96 95   5 4 3 2 1

Cover Design: The Visual Group

Library of Congress Cataloging-in-Publication Data
Ascher, William
    Communities and sustainable forestry in developing countries/
William Ascher.
        p.   cm.
    "A publication of the International Center for Self-Governance"—
Added t.p.
    Includes bibliographical references and index.
    ISBN 1-55815-419-1
    1. Community forests—Developing countries.   2. Sustainable
forestry—Developing countries.   3. Rural development—Developing
countries.   I. Title.
SD669.5.A83   1994
333.75'17'091724—dc20   94-29702
                                                         CIP

To Jane, Nancy, Sheila, and Valerie,
the core of my original community

Contents

Contents

A Note from the Publisher

In 1992 the International Center for Self-Governance published Elinor Ostrom's *Crafting Institutions for Self-Governing Irrigation Systems*, not intending at that time to initiate a series. Given the very strong and positive reaction to *Crafting*, however, we decided to create a series to make available further important works on this subject, and we persuaded Dr. Ostrom to become the series editor. With the publication of *Communities and Sustainable Forestry in Developing Countries*, we now officially launch the Self-Governing Communities series.

In this book, William Ascher explores an important policy question: How can we respond to the issue of deforestation so as to sustain our forests and at the same time maintain and even enhance the productive human activity that takes place in them? If we paid attention only to the conventional wisdom about forests and deforestation, we would think that the forested areas of the earth are dominated solely by centralized governments and large corporations. One of the major contributions of this book is that it deepens our understanding by introducing us to a much broader range of activities in forests and to the critical role that communities play in the use and health of forests worldwide.

Communities and Sustainable Forestry in Developing Countries explores a little-noticed aspect of forestry that is critical to the well-being of many people and many forests—how communities can establish governance systems that allow them to realize the goals of sustainable production necessary for their livelihood. This question raises serious theoretical and practical questions. The dominant interpretation of the tragedy of the commons erroneously presumes that the members of such a community would be rapacious users of forestry products and that only the intervention of a wise and benevolent government would stop the tragedy of depletion. Yet the answer Ascher provides is much different from the dominant theory and the conventional wisdom. He demonstrates that often the major culprits in deforestation are in fact national governments and that many times communities have devised innovative self-governing systems to create sustainable yields from their forest resources.

In self-governing ways of life, people are seen as more than clients and consumers. For community forest organizations, this means that the individuals involved are recognized as both producers and managers of the output of the forest and that they share a motivation to utilize the resource to its capacity without destructive exploitation. Because traditional users living in or near the forest have a stake in the outcome, they are frequently willing to modify and improve their methods of operation. The architects of community forest organizations often draw on refined methods of management that are compatible with the forest's long-term survival and make themselves personally responsible for the required labor, rules, and sanctions.

The role of government in conjunction with such organizations is crucial to their effectiveness. When there is no supportive partnership between the government and local community systems, the capacity of self-governing organizations to solve problems is destroyed. Government involvement, therefore, must be enabling rather than controlling. Studies on successful community problem solving—whether in effectively managing forest resources, solving overdrafts of water basins, or creating productive communities in public housing—point to one key element: recognition of the minimal yet fundamental right to self-organization.

The International Center for Self-Governance is confident that *Communities and Sustainable Forestry in Developing Countries* contributes essential lessons for redirecting environmental practices and will be welcomed as an informative resource for all those concerned with the future of our planet's forests.

ROBERT B. HAWKINS, JR.
President
Institute for Contemporary Studies

Foreword

It is with great pleasure that I have agreed to become the editor of a series of volumes on "Self-Governing Communities" for the Institute for Contemporary Studies and ICS Press. William Ascher's *Communities and Sustainable Forestry in Developing Countries* is everything that an editor would like to see as the first volume of a new series. Ascher addresses a subject area—the problem of achieving sustainable forests—which is at the top of many policy analysts' concerns. He draws on extensive empirical research to illustrate the critical importance of self-governing communities to the achievement of sustainable forests. He adds to our theoretical understanding of why those who are immediately dependent upon forest resources for their own survival are essential participants in devising rules and programs of activities to sustain these life-giving natural resources. And, he writes in a lively and readable fashion that can be read by busy officials, undergraduate and graduate students, research scholars, as well as by those who are the subject of his analysis, the users of forest resources.

In our contemporary times, most forest users who have themselves been responsible for the sustainability of forest and other natural resource systems for centuries, lack clear claims to property rights. Their claims to the use of land on which forests are located or to the flow of products from these forests are frequently clouded. By customary standards, they have developed rights to the continued use of forest resources due to their long-term use and development of these resources. Current governments tend not to recognize these customary rights and have in many instances declared forest lands to be government property. By trying to exclude customary users,

governments who themselves lack sufficient resources to protect local property rights, to plant and sustain degraded lands,
and to manage sustainable harvesting practices, turn away
the very people who might contribute most to the long-term
sustainability of biodiverse forest resources.

Ascher's analysis does not lead to a false dichotomy between local organization, on the one hand, versus government,
on the other. Ascher is intent on showing that both small-scale
and large-scale (and private, as well as public) forms of organization are essential in coping with the wide-ranging benefits
generated from effective governance and management of forest resources. The question is not whether local users can organize to replace the role of large-scale government entities
but how assigning secure rights to protect the interests of local
users can enhance their capabilities to organize and complement the activities and objectives of larger-scale public organization. The question is how to get rid of the many disincentives
leading local users to ignore long-term benefits achievable
through organization and investment. Creating incentives
leading toward greater net benefits, however, is not an easy
task in the forestry sector given the immense diversity of forest products, the complexity of forest ecosystems, and the
mixed time horizons, some of which are very long, involved in
achieving an appropriate mix of sustainable product flows.
While Ascher provides many useful principles that can be
used by government and forest users as they attempt to build
better incentives at all scales of organization, he carefully av-
oids oversimplifying these challenging tasks.

As a student of self-organizing institutions, I have learned
a great deal from this book. I commend it to all others, practi-
tioners and scholars alike, for whom self-governing societies
are important. It is especially worthwhile for those concerned
with problems of achieving sustainable natural resources in a
world of ever-increasing extractive demands.

ELINOR OSTROM
Codirector, Workshop in Political
Theory and Policy Analysis
Indiana University

Acknowledgments

The idea for a book presenting the basic design principles for community forestry management in developing countries came out of a meeting of the advisory board of the International Center for Self-Governance, a component of the Institute for Contemporary Studies. ICS has been a pioneer in bringing pragmatism and level-headed analysis to the study of public policies in developing countries. Under the able leadership of Elise Paylan Schoux, ICSG has married this pragmatism with the crucial idea of community self-empowerment. Inspired by earlier ICSG publications, including Elinor Ostrom's *Crafting Institutions for Self-Governing Irrigation Systems* (ICS Press 1992), this project was launched in the hope that the issues of community organization, risk-reducing business strategies, government relations with communities, and sustainable forestry development could be merged and conveyed in a coherent, straightforward fashion, so that they would be accessible to community-group leaders and government officials.

The research project from which this and other, more technical publications will emerge was undertaken by the author and Professor Marie Lynn Miranda, also of Duke University's Center for International Development Research, through funding from ICSG and Duke University's Center for Tropical Conservation. The financial support of the U.S. Agency for International Development (USAID), which funds both ICSG and Duke University's Center for Tropical Conservation, is gratefully acknowledged.

The broad research project and this book try to merge design principles with the real-world experiences of forest users.

Therefore the corps of researchers who contributed case study analyses and other research assistance to this project proved invaluable. They were Anjali Acharya, Maya Ajmera, Christopher Jones, Catherine Karr, Sharon LaPalme, and Sonal Tejani.

In June 1993, ICSG and Duke University's Center for International Development Research cosponsored a symposium on "Communities and Sustainable Forestry" to critique an earlier draft of this book and to engage in wide-ranging discussions of the challenges of community forestry management. The contributions of the symposium participants, Gustavo Arcia (Research Triangle Institute), Mimi Becker (Duke University), Shawn Bennett (Organization for Tropical Studies), David Bray (Inter-American Foundation), Garry Brewer (University of Michigan), Fred Cubbage (U.S. Forest Service), Karlyn Eckman (University of Minnesota), Sam Harper (ICS), Robert Hawkins (ICS), Kevin Healy (Inter-American Foundation), Robert Healy (Duke University), Julie Johnson (Duke University), Jan Laarman (North Carolina State University), Owen Lynch (World Resources Institute), Elise Paylan Schoux (ICSG), Priya Shyamsundar (Duke University), Elizabeth Station (Duke University), Toddy Steelman (Duke University), Carel van Schaik (Duke University), Christopher Welna (Duke University), and Mary Young (Research Triangle Institute) may be more worthy of publication than the book. The feedback from the symposium participants was extremely important for developing greater sensitivity to the issues of authority over assigning forest user rights, addressing environmental effects, and overcoming the risks of long-term forest development. Thoughtful comments on earlier drafts of the book were also provided by Marilyn Hoskins (FAO), Richard Norgaard, (University of California, Berkeley), Elinor Ostrom (Indiana University), and Anthony Pryor (USAID).

Despite all of these contributions, the errors and interpretations of the book remain the responsibility of the author.

1   Communities and Sustainable Forestry

The survival and quality of forests in most developing countries depend on the strength of community forestry organizations formed by the people traditionally involved in forest use. These organizations, with help—rather than control—from the government, are essential for promoting forest development and limiting forest extraction.

Some government officials and conservationists have found it difficult to accept the importance of traditional forest users. To many people, forests are conceived as apart from human effort. Some see forests as existing in majestic isolation, requiring the exclusion of people. Others view forests as dangerous haunts of snakes and wild beasts, as abandoned lands without "better" uses of agriculture or grazing. In some Latin American countries, for example, forestland is termed *tierra sucia*—"dirty land." A related attitude is that forests represent timber awaiting removal so that forestlands could be put to these other uses.

Yet these views are gradually giving way to a radically different understanding. In today's world, a forest is likely to be the site of intense human activity and probably must be so to survive the pressures of deforestation. Forests increasingly are places where a wide diversity of people try to earn their livelihoods, to provide for such necessities of life as fuel and food, or at least to supplement their incomes. "Forest systems" consist of people as much as they consist of plants and animals. To deny this reality, rather than to accept the need to allow human forest activity as long as it is within the bounds

1

of sustainability, risks undisciplined exploitation of forest resources.

The increased level of human activity in the forest has come about for at least four reasons. First, population growth has pushed people—sometimes through their own initiative, sometimes through governmental programs—into areas that were not previously preferred for human habitation. Likewise, the need to feed more people has pushed farming and cattle raising onto forestlands, even onto soils that cannot support agriculture or livestock sustainability. Increasing needs for fuelwood and other forest products have also increased the economic attractiveness of extracting these resources from the forest. Where the slash-and-burn agriculture of small groups of forest-dwellers had modest impacts erased by natural regeneration, larger groups now make a more lasting mark on the forests.

Second, technology has magnified the impact of people on forests. One man with a chain saw can fell more trees than twenty men using handsaws. Large expanses of natural forest have been replaced by tree species altered in the laboratory, cloned in high-tech nurseries, or brought in from different ecosystems. In some places the technologies of tree plantations have increased the intensity of human involvement in forests, but they reduce the variety of resources available for other people. Technology has given people the capacity to change the nature of the forest in very short periods and in dramatic ways.

Third, since forests are much more than just trees, they attract people interested in extracting or exploiting a remarkable range of products and services. The forests contain such diverse products as timber, fuelwood, game, rare butterflies and birds, palm fronds for floral arrangements, cultivated crops grown among the trees, etc. Even timber trees provide nonwood resources that are frequently exploited by people, including pine resin, latex, fruits and nuts, edible leaves, and thatch. The land on which the trees stand is, of course, another attraction for people. In addition, the forest provides employment for tour guides, park officers, and hunting guides. A careful look at the forest often reveals a complicated mosaic of different kinds of people using a wide array of resources found there.

Fourth, in addition to those who directly extract forest resources, others are interested in *restricting* its uses. The actions of forest conservationists, whether admired or resented, have complicated the politics of forest policy and have involved, directly or indirectly, an enormous number of people who may rarely come into direct contact with forests. This does not reduce their rights to be heard, however, since virtually everyone is affected by the goods and services produced by forests, from the air we breathe to the materials in our homes.

Since most forest systems involve so many human activities that may either complement or conflict with one another, the key challenge is to *organize these human activities.*

The Seriousness of the Problems

In many countries, the demands for timber and the demands to convert forestland into farms, mining sites, or pasture have put enormous pressures on the forests. As a result, forests have been shrinking. The overall statistics—that the world's forests shrank at a rate of 1.8 percent a year from the late 1970s to the late 1980s[1]—hide some dramatic declines in many developing countries that depend on forests for exports, industry, fuelwood, and protection of water systems. Going beyond the statistics to look at specific cases, we see very troubling combinations of declines in natural forests and failures to make up for these losses through planting programs.

Even using official government information, which often underestimates the loss of forests, many countries have experienced dramatic deforestation (see Table 1). In Latin America, Haiti lost half of its forests from 1980 to 1990, Costa Rica and Paraguay lost nearly one-third, and Honduras lost almost one quarter. Ecuador, Guatemala, Nicaragua, and Panama lost roughly one-fifth of their natural forests. Spanning the same decade in Africa, Malawi lost 15 percent of its forests, while Ghana, Guinea, Ivory Coast, the Sudan, Tanzania, Uganda, and Zambia lost more than one-tenth. In Asia, Bangladesh lost almost half of its forests, and Pakistan, the Philippines, and Thailand lost close to 40 percent in the same ten-year period. In addition, Malaysia lost more than one-fifth of its natural forests, and Vietnam lost nearly one-sixth (Food

3

TABLE 1
Forestry Trends in Developing Countries

Country	Natural forest (1,000 hectares) in 1990	Percentage change from 1980 to 1990	Percentage change in sawnwood production 1977–79 to 1987–89	Percentage change in panel production 1977–79 to 1987–89
Africa				
Angola	23,074	−7.2	−88	−75
Botswana	14,261	−5.1	na	na
Cameroon	20,350	−6.1	+58	+10
Central African Republic	30,562	−4.1	−40	−20
Congo	19,865	−2.0	+12	−26
Ethiopia	14,165	−3.0	−46	+10
Gabon	18,235	−6.1	+17	+75
Ghana	9,555	−13.8	+10	−11
Guinea	6,692	−12.7	0	−100
Ivory Coast	10,904	−10.5	+15	+133
Kenya	1,187	−6.2	+25	+172
Liberia	4,633	−5.1	+129	−44
Madagascar	15,782	−8.3	0	+467
Malawai	3,486	−14.9	−27	+13
Mozambique	17,329	−7.2	−59	+113
Namibia	12,569	−3.0	na	na
Nigeria	15,634	−7.2	+70	+102
Senegal	7,544	−7.2	+32	na
Somalia	754	−4.1	0	−33
Sudan	42,976	−11.6	−7	−40
Tanzania	33,555	−12.7	+78	+39
Uganda	6,346	−10.5	+10	+233
Zaire	113,275	−6.2	+4	+109
Zambia	32,301	−11.6	+61	+92
Zimbabwe	8,897	−7.2	+22	−11
Latin America				
Bolivia	49,317	−12.7	−44	−76
Brazil	561,107	−6.2	+36	+29
Colombia	54,064	−7.2	−24	+3
Costa Rica	1,428	−33.1	−12	−18
Ecuador	11,962	−19.5	+65	+114
Guatemala	4,225	−18.4	−70	−42
Guyana	18,416	−1.0	−9	na
Haiti	23	−59.8	0	na
Honduras	4,605	−23.1	−27	−32
Mexico	48,586	−13.8	+8	+79
Nicaragua	6,013	−20.7	−45	−64
Panama	3,117	−20.7	+7	−18
Paraguay	12,859	−30.5	+120	+253

TABLE 1 *(Continued)*

Country	Natural forest (1,000 hectares) in 1990	Percentage change from 1980 to 1990	Percentage change in sawnwood production 1977–79 to 1987–89	Percentage change in panel production 1977–79 to 1987–89
Peru	67,906	−4.1	+14	−27
Suriname	14,768	−1.0	−15	−61
Venezuela	45,690	−12.7	−6	+89
Asia				
Bangladesh	769	−46.6	−54	−75
India	51,729	−6.2	+93	+98
Indonesia	109,549	−10.5	+191	+1,635
Laos	13,173	−9.4	−66	+800
Malaysia	17,583	−21.9	+20	+66
Myanmar	28,856	−13.8	−20	+25
Nepal	5,023	−10.5	0	na
Pakistan	1,855	−39.7	+1,185	+113
Philippines	7,831	−38.4	−35	−21
Thailand	12,735	−38.4	−30	+82
Vietnam	8,312	−16.1	−40	+58

SOURCE: FAO 1993 and WRI 1992.

and Agriculture Organization 1993). The actual loss may be much worse, since these figures rarely take into account that some still-forested areas have been badly degraded. This is seen in the sparseness of vegetation and the scarcity of trees of value for timber or for nontimber extraction such as latex or Brazil nuts. It is also seen in the decline of the environmental benefits of forests, such as anchoring the soil to prevent soil erosion and flooding, providing suitable habitats for local wildlife, and even stabilizing the climate.

Of course, not all forests need to be preserved. If land could be put to better economic use, taking into account the environmental protection that forests provide (such as keeping soil in place, reducing the chances of flooding, and providing habitats for animals and plants), then converting forestlands to agriculture, pasture, industry, or residential areas can make perfect sense. After all, forestry is not an activity that usually yields high incomes; if other activities can yield higher incomes on a sustained basis, they will contribute more to overall economic returns. However, in most instances remaining

5

forestlands are "marginal" lands that are not well-suited to other activities. They often have poor soils, poor drainage, and remote locations. Land-use studies can determine how much land should remain as forest, both because of the benefits that forests bring and also because of the unsuitability for other pursuits such as agriculture and grazing.

The problem is that in many countries the area actually under forest cover has shrunk far below the area that has been determined to be best suited to forests. For example, in Guatemala less than half of the land classified as production forestland was actually forested as of 1984. As for land designated as "protected forest," only slightly more than half was actually forested (Abt Associates 1990c: II–9). In neighboring Honduras, 8.3 million hectares (or three-quarters of the national territory) is suited only for forestry, yet as of 1986 only 5 million hectares of this area was still forested, a deficit of nearly 40 percent (Abt Associates 1990d: 4, 8) In Indonesia, a far bigger country, 144 million hectares are supposedly forested and under the authority of the Forestry Ministry, yet the most reliable estimates are that forests cover only roughly 98 million hectares (Schwarz 1992: 61).

In some cases, the forest cover remains, but the economic value of the forest has been drained by the rapid removal of the most valuable trees. For example, in Belize, a thinly populated country of less than 200,000 people with an area of nearly 24,000 square kilometers, forests still cover the majority of the country, but at the present logging rates of mahogany and other commercial trees, timber producers would be out of business within a decade (Abt Associates 1990a). In Indonesia, there are estimates that all commercial timber will be gone within thirty years at the present rates of exploitation (Schwarz 1990: 62). Some prized furniture woods, such as *ramin*, are already scarce. Depletion of Indonesia's Sumatran forests has resulted in the need to import logs from Kalimantan to supply the Sumatran mills, and there are early indications that timber supplies are faltering even in the timber-boom areas of Kalimantan. Some Indonesian government officials estimate that, throughout the country, sawmills are operating at only an average of 40 percent capacity, although this is a reflection of poor siting of the mills as well as overall problems of supply. Nongovernmental estimates of commercial logging rates, in the range of 44 million cubic meters of wood, far exceed the government's own calculation that 31 million cubic meters is the maximum sustainable yield (Wahana Lingkungan Hidup Indonesia 1991).

Going beyond these statistics, we can ask what the decline of forests means to the people in these countries. For the people dependent on gathering fuelwood, it means an extraordinary amount of time spent on locating accessible trees. In the Tinan hills of Nepal it was already taking an average of three hours a day in 1978 to collect fuelwood, and in the Pangua hills it took four to five hours a day to gather one bundle. In the early 1980s it took this same amount of time to gather fuelwood in India's Chamoli hills and in the severely depleted areas of the Gujarat plains, while in the Garhwal hills it took five hours a day and an average trek of ten kilometers. In the arid Sahel region of Africa, it was estimated that in 1977 it took three hours a day for a family to gather fuelwood, and a 1981 estimate put it at three to four hours a day (Agarwal 1986).

Reliance on forests for job opportunities has also become a great risk. For the people who harvest wood and other products from the forest, the decline in forested areas and the quality of the forests has a direct and obvious effect on their livelihoods. In many countries, forests were supposed to serve as the base for industry. In every world region, major investments have gone into sawmills, plywood factories, furniture factories, and other wood-products industries. These have often grown up rapidly when governments permit large-scale logging. Yet in many instances the investments are squandered as the timber supply crashes because of previous overexploitation. In Angola, the Central African Republic, Ethiopia, Mozambique, Bolivia, Guatemala, Nicaragua, Bangladesh, Laos, and Vietnam the production of sawn timber declined by 40 percent or more from the late 1970s to the late 1980s. In Angola, Liberia, the Sudan, Bolivia, Guatemala, Nicaragua, Suriname, Bangladesh, and Iran the production of plywood panels declined by at least 40 percent during that same period (World Resources Institute 1992: 288–89). Some countries, such as Indonesia and Pakistan, showed remarkable increases in production of sawn timber and plywood, but their expansion sows the seeds for the possibility of a later crash, which seems to be starting already in Indonesia.

Similarly, some nontimber forest products have suffered declines. Within the past several years the supply of rattan (a bamboo used for light-weight furniture) has dropped drastically, threatening the furniture industry in several countries and setting off a scramble for substitutes. *Xate* palm fronds from Guatemala, a valuable export for floral arrangements, have been declining because of overexploitation.

Some people have argued that the disappearance of natural forests is not such a serious problem, since plantations could fulfill the needs for timber, nontimber products such as rubber or resin, and even forest cover. Plantations seemed to hold out the promise of intensive, scientifically managed forestry. Not all trees have to be in forests. Some, if not all, of the benefits of forests can be achieved by less dense plantings, such as planting trees in strategic locations on farms (so-called agroforestry), or less extensive plantings such as community woodlots. These options can provide some timber, some nontimber resources, and, in a modest way, contribute to preserving small wildlife.

The problem is that even plantations and less-extensive tree-planting programs have failed in many countries. In El Salvador, for example, the Forestry Service planted 20,000 hectares of trees since 1975, but as of 1990 only 7,000 hectares remained forested (Abt Associates 1990b: 64).

Why has the reforestation effort fallen so short of achieving its goals? There are three reasons. First, people have not responded to the rewards that governments have tried to offer to plant and care for trees. In some cases, the rewards have been too small to induce people to try. Governments may want to brag about having reforestation programs, or to claim credit for the programs from the international donor community, but they may not be providing sufficient resources to make replanting and nurturing attractive. In other cases, the government designs the rewards poorly, so that people can claim the rewards without putting in the necessary work to bring the trees to commercial maturity. For example, in Costa Rica a large proportion of the tax credits offered for tree planting could be claimed before the full effort and expense went into growing the trees for a long enough period.

Second, many reforestation efforts have been based on the wrong selection of trees. Often "exotic" (non-native) fast-growing trees are permitted or even required, but they have frequently turned out to be easily stunted or killed off by local insects, plant diseases, weather, minerals in the soil, or insufficient water. The decisions that lead to the planting of the wrong types of trees reflect both an ignorance of science and a disregard of local people's knowledge about which native species grow well under what conditions.

Third, planted trees are not immune to being cut too soon, either by people who had nothing to do with growing them, or by the planters who find that they need immediate income. Governments that boast of millions of trees planted rarely keep track of how many actually escape premature harvesting.

This widespread deterioration is due to too many, and often conflicting, demands. Where land ought to remain as forest, these demands must somehow be limited and controlled. The survival and sustainability of these forests depend on inventing arrangements that can balance both the kinds and intensity of forest uses.

The question is *how*, given that existing efforts at limitation and control are failing in many places. One might say that efforts to control the demands have been half-hearted, and therefore it is simply an issue of trying harder. Yet the reality is that current arrangements, which usually involve governmental control, either have not produced sufficient effort at limiting and guiding forest uses or have produced strong efforts that nonetheless have failed. Indeed, strong efforts to keep people from using forests have often led to sharp conflicts and willful forest destruction.

In short, the ability of standard policies to prevent inappropriate deforestation, or to make up for it through government-sponsored replanting, is very doubtful. New approaches, getting to the root of people's motivations to develop and nurture forests responsibly, are clearly needed.

Communities and Sustainability

My argument is that local people with established patterns of forest use are the key to sustainability, if they can organize themselves into effective communities. They are often the most appropriate managers and regulators of forest uses for four reasons.

First, limiting the number of users can reduce the pressure on the forest resource. By community forestry, we mean the control over forest uses by a more-or-less well-defined group of people claiming customary use rights; we do not mean that everyone in a particular geographical area has access to the forest resources. Traditional forest users are typically few in number compared to the total number of potential forest users, and the intensity of their forest uses is modest or moderate. To the degree that a limited group can retain exclusive use of one or more forest resources, more sustainable practices are likely to be implemented.

Second, traditional forest users living in or near the forest site have an interest in the long-term sustainability of that forest, as long as they know that they can continue to enjoy the benefits of the forest. Unlike large-scale commercial loggers who can operate in many locations, people rooted to a particular locale by tradition and long-standing user rights cannot afford to deplete the local forest resources and simply move to an entirely new location. Even people engaged in slash-and-burn (or swidden) agriculture have to be concerned about the sustainability of the overall migration area, since it would be risky for them to try to move into entirely new areas where other groups may defend their own claims.

Third, if the government permits local forest users to police the forest, then effective regulation has a real chance. By their very nature, forests are difficult to patrol, but of all the possibilities for forest regulation, local people with established practices of moving through the forest—and who also have a strong interest in preventing others from abusing the forest—have the greatest potential for both capability and motivation to regulate effectively. Governments have often rushed in to assert their control over forests, claiming to be the most effective and legitimate regulators. In practice, governments have typically had a disastrous record in limiting forest uses, even by the government itself and its enterprises. There are usually great pressures on government either to exploit natural resources rapidly as a quick way to earn revenues, or to let commercial operations do so. In addition, governments often prefer to use the forest as an outlet for growing population rather than undertake a meaningful land reform. Government forestry officials often prefer to spend their time in the capital city, rather than face the privations and dangers of remote forest posts. Even those fully committed to maintaining the forest often lack the personnel and financial resources necessary to enforce the restrictions. In Costa Rica, for example, the General Forestry Directorate is frequently so underfunded that it cannot afford gasoline for its jeeps to move through the forest (Ascher 1993). People intent on encroaching into the forest often feel freer to target so-called state forest lands than forests under community forestry control, knowing that they would only run the risk of facing a few government forest guards rather than a whole community mobilized to protect its forest-use rights. When traditional forest users are subject to the same restrictions as other groups, they lose their incentive to exploit forest resources sustainably and sometimes make a crusade out of defying the government's restrictions.

Fourth, traditional forest users are generally more likely to have developed practices that are compatible with the long-term survival of the forest. Other groups, with less familiarity with the forest and with fewer tested techniques for extracting forest products, are more likely to engage in short-sighted practices.

Therefore the logic of community forestry goes far beyond the patronizing view that community forestry means letting the local people get some benefits from the forest, or from resources that the government provides to enhance the forest. Community forestry is not "social forestry" in the sense of government subsidy programs for forest users that the government designs and implements as part of its social welfare program for the disadvantaged. Yes, community forestry can improve the well-being of low-income people, but more importantly it can create and maintain a system of forest practices that are both ecologically and economically sustainable.

Community forestry has the potential to conserve forests that cannot be sustained if exploited by the society as a whole.

Who Are the Forest Users?

Whether this strategy of community control of forests is fair and effective depends on who the forest users are and whether they have appropriate incentives and capabilities to safeguard the forests and smaller stands of trees. As we shall see, changing conditions can lead traditional forest users to either intensify or abandon their uses. These conditions, including government policy, can also keep most other people away from forest use, induce them to enter into forest development, or induce them into unsustainable forest extraction.

Defining forest-resource users is more complicated than defining the users of other natural resource systems such as irrigation or fisheries. While those who cut down trees are by far the most visible, there are also exploiters of the innumerable types of by-products from the trees (nuts, fruits, resins, leaves, flowers, roots, fodder, fuelwood, etc.), as well as products from insects and animals that exist in forests. These non-timber products can be extracted either by those who hold the rights to harvest timber trees themselves, or by others, depending on the user rights recognized by law or custom. Then there are the people who create or maintain artificial forests, whether these are large-scale plantations (for timber or other forest products) or modest village woodlots. This is another reflection of the complexity of forest systems, and its many potential uses.

The users include:

- timber cutters—those who own the land, obtain the rights to cut trees, or do so without legal or customary permission; those who harvest trees from natural forests, plantations, or community woodlots

- forest plantation workers

- community woodlot overseers

- gatherers of poles from immature trees—who sell the poles as construction materials that do not require milling—in many countries

- fuelwood gatherers in countries as diverse as India, Haiti, and Nigeria

- *xate* palm gatherers in the Peten (northeastern) region of Guatemala (*xateros*)—these fronds are exported to florists in many countries

- pine resin tappers in Honduras

- durian fruit gatherers in Indonesia

- gum acacia (chicle) tappers in Central America (*chicleros*)

- rubber tree tappers in Amazonian countries (*caucheros*) and Southeast Asia

- tourist guides—and tourists—in Costa Rica (and many other countries)

- game hunters—in Liberia, for example, it has been estimated that roughly 80 percent of the rural population's animal protein comes from the forest (ITTO 1988: 48)

- Brazil nut gatherers in Brazil and Peru

- herders, who rely on forest areas for fodder

- corn planters in Mexico, who rely on the nutrients released by burning the forest

- cassava (or manioc) growers in many African, Asian, and Latin American countries, who raise their crops among forest trees

- prospectors and miners, who know that minerals are often found in forested areas [2]

Even this incomplete list shows how diverse the users of forest resources can be. It shows that people living within forested areas, or in areas capable of being forested, may have many options open to them, whether or not they are traditional forest users. As we shall see, this raises a surprising but serious problem. When governments introduce additional benefits into forestry activities, people who otherwise would have little interest in forestry may choose to become involved. At first glance this may seem like a good thing—if we could assume that they would devote their efforts to forest development activities like tree planting. Yet even tree-planting programs can have negative outcomes, as when natural forests are removed and harmful exotic species are planted. More important, any actions that make the forest sector an attractive money-making possibility may bring too many exploiters into the forests. This is especially serious when the newcomers lack the necessary skills and commitment to sustainability that long-standing forest involvement normally brings.

General characteristics of forest users and their predicament.

Despite the diversity of people working with forest resources, there are some more-or-less general characteristics of forest users that reinforce the points previously made.

First, most forest users rely on the forest for only part of their income. Aside from full-time workers of commercial logging companies and government forestry officials, forest exploitation represents *supplemental* income—although this additional income may be extremely important. And except for very tiny populations of forest-dwellers living in unchanged traditional ways, the people who gather forest products (such as fuelwood, fruits, or game) for their own use also rely on the forest for only part of their subsistence. As a result, forest exploitation may well *not* be a necessary activity of many of the people who could or do exploit forest resources. Forest users are often engaged more intensively in other productive activities, such as farming, while their exploitation of forest resources is seasonal or occasional. Honduran resin tappers, for example, are typically smallholder farmers who spend two to three days a week during the six-month tapping season to install tubes and drain cups and collect the resin (Stanley 1991: 31). The *xate* palm gatherers of Guatemala are also largely farmers who make periodic expeditions into the forest to gather the fronds, usually exiting as quickly as possible to minimize their exposure to biting insects and poisonous snakes. Nut and fruit gathering is, of course, a largely seasonal undertaking; in some cases, such as gathering the durian fruit of Indonesia, it does not even occur every year. Tree planting and weeding also require only part-time effort, although the low intensity of effort is offset by the long periods needed until trees can be harvested.

The part-time nature of forest exploitation means that, for most involved, it will be a supplemental activity. Unlike farming, herding, or fishing, forest development and exploitation do not predominantly define the social or economic role of those who undertake it in this part-time fashion. Farmers typically tend to their irrigation systems as a matter of obvious importance. Forest users, however, may simply lose their incentive to enhance and protect the forest. As a result, the forest that is not being used for resource extraction is an easy target for massive timber harvesting. Extractors are not available to press for their legal or customary rights to continue to extract resources from the intact forest, and the government is unlikely to regard the nontimber value of the forest as being significant enough to offset the economic gains of harvesting the timber.

The second general characteristic of traditional forest users is that they usually have low incomes. To be sure, there are millionaire logging barons. Yet the individuals involved in going into the forest to grow, gather, guide, or cut tend to be people with few alternatives for earning supplemental income. Many rely on gathering from the forest to meet their own needs because they lack the disposable income to purchase fuelwood, building materials, etc., from the market. Forestland is generally not good farmland, and unless an individual has large tracts of forestland, the income yielded from timber and nontimber resources is usually quite modest compared to the income-earning activities of most other people. Thus, while trees can be valuable assets, and extracting nontimber resources from forests can be an important income supplement, forest activities make few people rich or even middle income by the standards of their countries.

The generally low-income status of traditional forest users is a crucial fact in justifying efforts to give these people more-or-less exclusive rights to continued forest use. The moral logic is that in many cases the forest simply does not have enough resources for everyone to exploit, even among the poor. This can be seen most clearly in countries such as India and other parts of South Asia, and in other countries with high population densities from El Salvador in Central America to Rwanda in central Africa. Even where forest use has been dominated by very poor people, the forest has not been able to survive exposure to so many of the poor, even if they are all deserving of an opportunity to gain income or to fill some of their immediate needs for food and fuel from the forest. There are bare, lifeless hills in these countries where forests once stood, even in areas where the wealthy never bothered to try to exploit the forests. The issue of limiting access to the forest, then, is not necessarily a question of excluding the poor for the sake of the rich or the government, but rather a question of deciding what limited portion of poor ought to be able to use the forest in a sustainable way. As long as the traditional forest users are part of the low-income population, there is no ethical problem for them to be the ones who have rights to use the forests while others are excluded.

Indeed, there are ethical reasons to acknowledge that their claims are morally stronger than those of migrants or of other local groups who had no previous pattern of forest use. Insofar as the traditional forest users have already adapted their work and lives to the opportunities of using the forest, supplanting them with others would create the greatest likely deprivation. Migrants and other groups intent on using the forest may have equally great needs, but they face the need to change their economic practices in any event. Why subject the forest users to wrenching changes unnecessarily? Some aspects of cultural survival are often at stake. Cultural practices usually come along with these economic practices; why force changes upon the only group whose culture has developed on the basis of forest use? In terms of the legitimacy of rights, customary forest use does represent one basis for claiming the right to continued use of the forest. If other groups are no more deserving in terms of their neediness, this basis for claiming rights remains unchallenged by other claims of rights. Finally, surviving forests often reflect past restraint on the part of the ancestors of today's forest users. If the self-sacrifice of these ancestors (or the living forest users up to now) was intended to safeguard the forest for their children, is it fair to undermine their sacrifice by handing the forest over to others?

The third defining characteristic of forest users is that they generally lack clear, formal property rights over the trees and the forestland, whether they are extracting timber or other forest resources. That is, they do not hold title over the trees (which may be held by the state, by other individuals, by other communities, or by no one), and their cutting of the trees may be legally prohibited, with greater or lesser effectiveness. Yet even without government-sanctioned ownership, these forest users may have forest rights recognized by their communities. This issue is discussed at length in Chapter 2.

User-rights combinations show remarkable variety. The Honduran government has recognized the right of certain groups to tap the resin from pine trees, although the trees are owned by the state and the land by either the state or by private owners (this right is now jeopardized, as discussed later). In Japan, certain groups had the right to harvest only one or a few specific tree species from land owned by others (McKean 1982).

Obviously, one of the main threats to forest users is that changes in government-assigned property rights would exclude or reduce their uses of the forest. When forestland is put into private hands, the private owner may decide that other forest users ought to be kept off the land, whether because the private owner fears that they will destroy the trees or that they will bring the issue of legal ownership into question. Legal systems often lack the flexibility to assign community-based property rights. When forestland is put under state ownership, or when state ownership is more vigorously enforced, laws and policing against trespass and poaching are often increased. Governments, in trying to exclude people who would contribute to deforestation, often end up excluding people who would have engaged in benign or sustainable extraction of nontimber resources or would have contributed through replanting efforts.

The Objectives of Organizing for Forest Use: Motivation and Exclusion

These characteristics of forest users and their predicaments make it clear that forest users need to be organized for two essential purposes: to motivate ongoing forest use and to restrict overuse.

On land that is best suited for forests but is currently without many trees, the obvious challenge is to organize for planting and maintaining trees. While in some cases tree planting has been portrayed as a single burst of communal energy to put seeds or saplings in the ground, in actuality the survival of trees in plantations or community woodlots requires sustained, painstaking care and restraint from premature or excessive exploitation. Both the effort and the restraint can only come from shared community commitment.

On currently forested land, the organizational challenge is more complicated. Sustainable timber extraction requires organization, but so too does the sustainable extraction of nontimber resources. Organizing to impose restraint is even more important if the forest provides other benefits, such as preservation of species or the maintenance of water quality. In some natural forests, the community may even be called upon to enrich natural growth with some tree plantings.

Thus the following requirements arise:

Motivating ongoing forest use.

The first requirement for maintaining forests and smaller stands of trees is to ensure that *individuals and groups are motivated to grow trees, and to exploit the forest's nontimber resources, on an ongoing basis.* This requirement seems at first glance to be contradictory. It is surprising, from a conservation point of view, that it is important to provide people with reasons to chop down trees, prune branches, extract palm fronds, capture butterflies, etc., from the forests that conservationists regard as already under too much pressure. Yet these opportunities for economic gain or contributions to meeting everyday needs are what give the forests their *value* in the eyes of the society and the government. Harvesting, especially if done with discipline and combined with resource development (such as replanting), can be sustainable. Without opportunities for harvesting, many people do not care about sustainability and have little reason to be disciplined or to contribute to developing rather than extracting forest resources.

In many cases the question is not whether to have an exploited forest or a highly protected forest, but rather whether there will be a forest at all. If a forest does not provide sufficient value, it is much more vulnerable to conversion to other land uses: agriculture, pastureland, human settlement, etc. In many instances, forestland starts out with the stigma of being regarded as the lowest (or residual) use of land, implying that only land unsuitable for anything else should be left forested. It turns out that in many countries there is so much land with poor soil, steep slopes, or lack of water that indeed no other activities are suitable. Yet even in such cases there are many private efforts and government initiatives to try to convert forests into something else in the hopes that more productive purposes could be pursued. This is why so much land classified for forestry as its highest use in Central America, Brazil, Indonesia, and other countries has now been given over to low-return agriculture and grazing (Abt Associates 1990c, 1990d; Fearnside 1983; Schwarz 1992). This is much more likely to be attempted when the forest resources are not fully utilized.

Potentially valuable forest resources may have little actual value unless the government or other organized groups can create the circumstances that make the resources valuable. Working with forest resources—often wearying, dirty, and dangerous work—has to be not only profitable, but more profitable than other alternatives. When forest exploitation does not promise such profitability, the forest *as a forest* will be underused, but the chances of conversion to other land uses increases. For example, if sawmills and export facilities can only handle a limited number of species, other tree species may not be worth harvesting—and therefore not worth growing or protecting. Tapping resin from pine trees or latex from rubber trees may not be profitable if tappers' cooperatives do not pool resources to purchase trucks and processing equipment, or pool manpower to fend off encroachment by outsiders.

Finally, an important element of the requirement is that

19

people be motivated to use forest resources on an ongoing basis. This is another way of saying that there must be incentives for people to commit themselves to exploiting forest resources sustainably: a balance of enthusiasm and restraint must be encouraged. This can only be done if future economic rewards from forest exploitation appear as attractive as the possible income from go-for-broke, maximum, immediate exploitation.

Discouraging overuse and misuse.

The second requirement for sustaining forests is closely related to this need for ongoing, sustainable forest exploitation. It is the *importance of discouraging overuse and misuse of the forest resources*. Organization is often needed to prevent overexploitation from destroying the resource base. This is true even when exploitation is entirely within the traditional community. There are cases of overexploitation of forest resources that are only extracted by the traditional community; for example, the palm fronds (*xate*) that grow in the Guatemalan forests are beginning to show lower densities, and the harvests of tree bark and *illipe* nuts in Kalimantan, Indonesia, appear to be problematic (Salafsky, Dugelby, and Terborgh 1993: 44).

Discouraging overuse goes beyond ensuring that those entitled to use a forest resource will use it within bounds; it also requires that other people often must be kept from using the forest resource altogether. Excluding people may be a troubling measure, but it is necessary for many forest systems. The problem is that the self-restraint necessary for sustainable exploitation by any particular individual or group does not make sense if an unlimited number of other people could come in to extract the remaining resources. The individual logic is that, "If I don't get it now, someone else will." There is overwhelming evidence that "open-access" rules, whether formal or informal, result in overexploitation. Therefore the cold reality is that for forests to survive, someone must be excluded from forest use. The challenge for the society is to determine how to decide on inclusion and exclusion in a fair and productive way. Thus there is a dual challenge to organizing to discourage overuse: imposing discipline on those with access to the forest resource and excluding those without the right to access.

The Importance of Organizing

The intensity of forest uses has increased the risk that people will clash over their plans and actions to exploit forest resources. Some of these clashes are over competition for the same resource: logging companies and local communities wrestling over the rights to cut timber. Other clashes are over competition among different uses of the trees, land, or other forest resources: timber cutting versus resin tapping; cattle grazing or slash-and-burn agriculture versus tree exploitation; national parks for tourists versus intensive logging or agricultural conversion. Yet other clashes pit exploitation against preservation, as in the case of logging versus wildlife sanctuaries. The prevalence of these clashes makes it unreasonable to expect that independent or uncoordinated activity is consistent with maintaining peace among competitive forest users.

Government regulation, the apparent shortcut to resolving these competing demands, has often failed. In developing countries, government regulations on resource uses are often ignored, defied, twisted, or left unenforced. Indeed, a very strong regulation "on paper" is frequently a tip-off of nonenforcement—a sign that the government is trying to make up for, through rhetoric, what it has trouble doing concretely through action. The limitations on the effectiveness of regulation are the best evidence that people must be motivated, persuaded, and organized so that they want to do what regulations would try to require them to do.

The preceding requirements for sustaining forests emerge from the weakness of individuals acting alone. Single individuals often lack the resources to create the conditions needed to motivate ongoing forest exploitation, and they often lack the will and capacity to rein in their own and their neighbors' overuse of the resources. Two more requirements follow from this:

Nongovernmental collective action.

To carry out many of the actions necessary to encourage forest use but discourage overuse, *collective action outside of the government* is another essential requirement. The importance of both economic self-interest and of pooling resources makes it crucial that user groups act collectively. A user group can be defined as the people who have the rights, legally or by custom, to exploit a particular area. Their pooling of resources can help considerably to make current and future forest use attractive. Only by banding together can they strengthen their chances to keep others out. Thus the rather small groups directly involved in resource exploitation, such as the people entitled to harvest timber from a particular forest tract, local cooperatives of resin or latex tappers, or community woodlot caretakers, need to be organized to press for the protection of their resources and to maintain restraint from overexploitation on the part of the members of the group. They have the most intense interest in coordinated action.

Larger groupings of these smaller organizations can serve other very important purposes. They can help to resolve boundary disputes among the smaller organizations and provide technical help. They can pool part of their resources to achieve greater creditworthiness. The ability of larger organizations to pool their political power can help to protect the smaller organizations from efforts to suppress them. These larger groupings can join with one another to form still larger organizations, at the provincial (or state) level, the national level, and even the international level.

A supportive government.

Government, of course, also represents collective action, and indeed its role in encouraging forest use and discouraging overuse is absolutely pivotal. But here, too, there is a tension. Based on numerous cases, we will argue that government involvement is both essential and very dangerous.

As important as it is for nongovernmental groups to be active, the government cannot be circumvented. It may seem as if governments are so often antagonistic to nongovernmental groups that it would be better for them to be completely in-sulated from government efforts. And it may be tempting to try to eliminate the possibility that government will find ways to enrich itself through unsustainable forest exploitation. But neither can be done by having nongovernmental groups "go it alone" without collaborating with government agencies from the local to the national levels—nongovernmental groups can-not operate in a vacuum. This is because of what the govern-ment can contribute, and also because many factors are inevitably under governmental control.

In terms of potential contributions, a competent and well-disciplined government can mediate or arbitrate disputes among nongovernmental institutions, maintain the official memory of agreements and property titles, provide technical assistance for nongovernmental groups, and provide roads and facilities to permit timber and other forest products to be brought to market.

In addition to facilitating the constructive work of commu-nity groups and other nongovernmental institutions, the gov-ernment is often the only institution that can address the problem that even if a community of forest users develops and extracts forest products in ways that are good for that group, there may be results of their actions that harm others beyond their group. There is no reason to expect that the group's inter-nal coooperation and discipline would be focused on this type of problem. In other words, if community control means self-regulation out of healthy self-interest, who can attend to the unhealthy consequences of forestry practices that are not di-rectly borne by the user groups responsible for the damage?

Two roles for government are possible. The more modest approach is for government to facilitate communication and cooperation among all the affected groups, in forestry and beyond, so that they can try to work out reasonable agree-ments to limit damaging one another. In many instances, how-ever, there are real limits to how far the groups suffering from harm caused by others can convince or bargain to get the con-ditions improved. Therefore there is the second approach of government taking on the function of regulating these nega-tive external consequences.[3] While still leaving the inter-nal matters of established forest user groups to the users themselves, regulating the external impacts is a rather restrained role for government, but one that justifies governmental regulation even in the eyes of many experts who are skeptical of other reasons for regulation.

A related, and still modest, additional role for government is to provide incentives for groups to improve forest resources in ways that will produce positive results for others even though the direct benefits to the improvers are not sufficient to justify their effort in terms of self-interest. In such cases it may be justified for government to provide subsidies for forest-resource improvements. It is important that these subsidies not be so great as to waste scarce government money to promote efforts that go beyond society's true needs. Excessive subsidies also run the risk of attracting people into forest development who have no real commitment to improving and maintaining the forest.

Finally, even if government does not take on any of these active roles concerning forestry activities, it has to make crucial decisions, through action or by default, on very important factors. Specifically, the government establishes who has legally recognized property rights, who has the rights to organize, and how serious conflicts will be approached. Government policies that do not necessarily seem directly relevant to forest activities turn out to have unavoidable impacts: the government's tax system will either encourage or discourage sustainable uses of resources, and the government's trade policy heavily influences the prices of timber and nontimber products.

The danger of government involvement, however, is that it may squeeze out nongovernmental collective action. The risk is that governments will so dominate the legal management of forest resources that nongovernmental collective action will either fail to emerge or will be ineffective. Sometimes governments try to organize forest users into forest-management units, giving these units the rights to forest exploitation, thus either denying these rights to privately formed groups or distracting the energies of forest users from such private groups. When this happens, there is a grave risk that the government's desire to remain in control will keep the users' organizations from becoming true representatives of the forest users themselves. Such organizations often either die, because of lack of interest and support from the users, or become thinly veiled agents for the government. As governments in developing countries rarely have the administrative capacity to keep encroachers out of the forest, government-only forest management often means that an open-access situation actually holds.

Therefore the final basic requirement is that *government must support rather than dominate nongovernmental collective action.* This requires self-discipline on the part of the government. Yet it also requires a sophisticated approach to encourage rather than dictate, which runs counter to most of the routines and understandings that governments create.

Summary

To put all the essential requirements into one statement, we might say that: *Sustainable forestry activities need to be encouraged and disciplined through nongovernmental collective action, aided by supportive, rather than domineering, governmental actions.*

In the following chapters, we try to explain and justify the four requirements that go into this complex statement. More importantly, we offer some principles for designing forestry practices and organizations to pursue these objectives.

The requirements also define the structure of the book. In Chapter 2 we address the requirement to encourage ongoing forest exploitation by focusing on user rights and their importance for sustainable exploitation. Chapter 3 focuses on the importance of reducing risk and uncertainty in order to encourage investment of effort and other resources in forestry. The requirement of imposing restraint is addressed first in Chapter 4, on community efforts to balance internal rewards and responsibilities, while at the same time organizing to prevent outsiders from encroaching on the community's forest-use rights. The requirement of imposing restraint is also addressed in Chapter 5, on the role of the government, which must balance enforcement of restrictions with the need to promote community forestry. Since most governments have to strive to overcome community mistrust based on previous tendencies of governments to eliminate or restrict community rights, the government's own restraints become a very important element of the role of government in assisting the development of community forestry.

2   User Rights, User Groups, and Sustainable Forest Management

In this chapter, different arrangements for establishing the rights to forest development, exploitation, and sharing of profits are assessed in terms of their potential for providing secure, profitable incomes through responsible use. Our argument is that the most basic requirements for motivating people to care for forests responsibly are their current prospects of using the forest profitably and the assurance that *they* will be able to continue to use the forest in the future. This means that assurance of current and future use by members of the community is crucial for the responsible participation of local people in forest exploitation. This chapter explores how confidence in future use is important for sustainable forest use, and how this confidence can be created and maintained. It also identifies the major threats to this confidence and assesses how different forms of user rights can contribute to overcoming these risks. Community user rights, as long as the communities also have the rights to decide on how forest resources will be used and transferred, emerge as the most promising arrangement.

Our position is quite different from that of many governments. In the past century, governments have shrunk communal forest rights in favor of private ownership or state ownership. The major reason given by governments for taking over the control of forests is their concern that if the government does not intervene or regulate, people will behave irresponsibly. Government policy toward forests in developing countries has largely been framed as the challenge of insulating the forest from exploitation by the people and assuring that the government can restrict people's uses even more in the future. Yet the implication of this approach—excluding people from the forests—is typically not fair, sensible, or possible.

Examples can be found all over the world. As early as 1897, the government of Thailand took over the control of forests in northern Thailand from the local Laotian chiefs. Just before World War I the Forestry Department reserved the harvest of valuable tree species such as teak to those who could obtain permits and pay the royalty fees. By the 1930s the government established reserved and protected forests, and by the 1960s virtually all of Thailand's forests were state-owned, with elaborate permit-based regulations covering exploitation (Feeny 1988). Yet the result has been continued deforestation, possibly worsened by the hostility of local people to the government's restrictions. David Feeny reports:

> In spite of provisions for obtaining permits for domestic use, there is considerable tension between the traditional Thai villager's view of forests and forest products as common property resources and official government policy. Villagers resent the cumbersome procedures and expenses (both formal and informal) involved in obtaining permits to harvest timber legally and often circumvent them. Circumvention is especially common in officially reserved forest areas where villagers frequently harvest timber and clear land for cultivation. . . . Reportedly villagers tend to avoid encroachments on officially unreserved forest areas, feeling that they are the "property" of influential persons and therefore violations will be detected and violators punished. (Feeny 1988: 125–26)

In the once-lush Kumaon forests of India's Uttar Pradesh state, government control imposed in the nineteenth century was initially under the jurisdiction of the conservation-minded Forest Department, which often enraged local people by excluding them from important forest uses on land that had previously been open to them. In the 1920s the colonial government took control out of the hands of the Forest Department—due to grievances by local people—and handed the administration over to the Revenue Department, which had little concern or expertise about forestry practices and favored commercial logging that brought in big royalty payments. These "Civil Forests" were then badly abused by both local people and commercial loggers, to the point where many "had hardly a tree on them by the 1960s when they were turned over either to village councils or once again to the Forest Department" (Tucker 1988: 97).

In Honduras, the national government declared *all* trees state property in 1974. The government's official management of its commercial pine forests has reflected a sustainable-yield philosophy, because the government's state forestry enterprise Corporación Hondureña de Forestería (COHDEFOR) earns its own budget from the pine harvests, and has been harsh in trying to keep local people from destroying trees. Yet the government's denial of user rights to local people contributes to their hostility not only toward the government, but also toward the forest:

> Nearby pine forests can be easily exploited by local farmers with a minimum risk of COHDEFOR control in most of the country . . . much of COHDEFOR activity is directed toward preserving the forest. The peasants, on the other hand, seem to have an indifferent and even hostile attitude toward this in general. The distance between these attitudes is a measure of the problems currently faced by social forestry. (Jones 1988: 157–58)

As a consequence, there is widespread removal of fuelwood, squatting by farmers on forestland claimed by the government, and illegal burning of forestland not only to plant crops, but also to extend pastures (Jones 1988: 157–58). The situation in Honduras's broadleaf forests, rich in game and other forms of biological diversity, is worse; they have been disappearing rapidly (Abt Associates 1990d), in part because COHDEFOR has little commercial interest in them and has devoted even fewer resources to their conservation.

In the southern African nation of Lesotho, communal land

devoted to woodlots was supposed to engage community effort, and proceeds were to go to the community. In the 1978 Forestry Act, however, the government of Lesotho asserted its authority to control and manage the woodlots and through this act claimed the bulk of the income from the woodlots. Reforestation efforts promoted by the government have been disappointing, in part because of the complexity and antagonisms over control and money—including the Forestry Department's delays in paying the villages their minority share of the proceeds (Turner 1988: 199–203).

One reason why governments have pursued failing efforts to conserve forests through state control is that government officials often act on the assumption that formal rules of ownership and rights—as set out by official laws and policies—are also the effective rules. They act as if people will accept these rules as appropriate simply because they are the official, governmental rules. Yet many people outside of government, if they observe rules of rights and ownership at all, will recognize the traditional or customary rights. These attitudes toward rights are developed within communities of people of common lineage, identity, and interests, and more broadly within geographical areas in which different groups buy, sell, share, or struggle over the rights to use the various forest resources in a given location. Therefore behind the apparent issue of "illegal" activity—people not following the formal rules—lies a more basic issue of who has the right to determine who should use the forest.

On the most practical level, the question is what arrangement of user rights, and what authority to decide on user rights, will improve the chances for sustainable forest uses. As outlined in Chapter 1, our argument is that traditional or customary user rights need *clear and secure* recognition and that the authority of communities to govern the forest uses of their members also requires clear and secure recognition.

We come to this conclusion because responsible management of forest resources, in terms of both development and exploitation, depends on clear and secure profit opportunities for the forest user. For forest *development*, profit opportunities are necessary because forest development is not a very attractive economic activity for many people. While there are some people with strong cultural commitments to planting trees, there are also many circumstances that do not make people willing to put backbreaking labor into planting trees, maintaining forest trails, or engaging in other forest development activities. Many of the positive qualities of trees—protecting soils, reducing flooding, providing habitat for a diversity of animals and plants—are general benefits for the society, but do not offer much direct incentive for whoever has to provide money and hard labor to enrich the forest. Generally there has to be profit, and the profit has to be greater than that to be gained from other ways that people can devote their resources and efforts. Tree-planting programs and collective efforts to establish trails to extract nontimber resources such as rubber or Brazil nuts are examples of resource developments that would receive little support without confidence on the part of the people involved that they would be able to reap benefits.

For forest *exploitation* to be responsible, forest users also have to be confident that gradual exploitation will not allow others to take what the user could exploit today. Too rapid or wasteful exploitation is often the result of desperate efforts to gain income while the exploiter still has the access. For future use to be securely profitable, other potential extractors must be excluded. Except for the resources of such low value that no one else is interested in exploiting them, the profitability of forest resources depends on reserving them for particular users. Assurances for one user group often mean exclusion of others; this is why determining who can use forest resources is so often a political issue. When limiting the number of exploiters is important for keeping exploitation at a reasonable rate, exclusion is an essential requirement.

Finally, communities and governments ought to be concerned not only with how well the forests do, but also with the fairness of who shares in the profits from their exploitation. Putting backbreaking hours into planting trees or walking the snake-infested trails to gather palms, rubber, or nuts is not reward in itself. The ultimate question is who prospers from forest exploitation. Sharing the income depends not only on who actually exploits the resources, but also on who can buy the forest products from the original exploiter, who sets the price, and who can claim a share of the profits whether or not involved in direct forest development and exploitation.

In short, communities and policy makers must be concerned about assurances of use because these assurances determine:

1. how enthusiastically people will *develop* forest resources
2. how carefully people will *extract* forest resources
3. how *fairly* the income from forest resources will be shared

In examining different arrangements of forest user rights and their impacts on responsible use, we focus on the risks that the developer and exploiter face in trying to gain secure, profitable incomes. Our assumption is that arrangements that can reduce these risks will be best for encouraging responsible forest use.

Rights and Risks

The key question now is how different types of user rights affect the assurances that forest users will be able to continue to have profitable access to the forest. The best way to look at this is to examine the risks that forest users face and how severe these risks are under different user-rights arrangements.

The risks to profitable forest use are:

1. *Others' access.* Others will extract resources that the forest user was planning to extract at a future date—either resources that developed naturally or were developed by the forest user. This may occur because the forest is open to access by many other users, or because the government grants user rights to another set of users.

2. *Stricter regulation.* The forest user's capacity to extract the resources will be limited by the government. That is, the government may change its rules in regulating resource extraction, possibly in the name of conservation.

3. *Exclusion by other "owners."* The forest user's capacity to extract the resources will be limited by others who claim to "own" the land on which the resources are located.

4. *Low share of communal earnings.* The forest user will receive too small a share of the communal income.

5. *Low credit.* The forest user will be unable to obtain the credit needed to develop the forest to the point where attractive profits could be obtained. This is particularly serious when the forest resource itself cannot be offered as collateral to secure a loan.

6. *Cash shortage.* The forest user will be short of cash to pay for urgent needs (such as food, family medical treatment, or education) because income that otherwise would be available is tied up in forest resources that cannot yet be sold profitably. This, too, can be the result of the inability to use the forest resource as collateral to obtain a loan. It also occurs when the forest user cannot sell the rights to the future harvest or the rights to the forest use itself.

7. *Low market prices.* The forest user will be unable to obtain a high enough price for the products extracted from the forest. Sometimes market conditions change, turning what had been a profitable forest venture into an unprofitable one. Often government actions are behind such changes. Sometimes the government reduces prices directly through price controls. The crucial point here is that "ownership" can have little meaning when the capacity to earn income from the resource is denied the "owner" by government policy to set prices below levels that permit a profit. [1]

8. *Spillover effects.* The ability to extract profitable incomes from the forest will be endangered by the side effects of activities of other forest exploiters. For example, loggers may destroy trees that yield nontimber products such as latex or nuts, mining may destroy timber, and tourism may scare away game.

Rights and Ownership

To assess which user-rights arrangements will reduce these risks, it is important to understand that there is a wide range of rights for any given resource. This fact is obscured by the more common idea of property ownership, which implies that virtually the whole bundle of user rights is placed in the hands of a single actor, whether it be an individual, family, group, company, or government. It further implies that the "owner" can treat the land in any way he or she prefers. Many laws, and most of the programs to provide clear titles, operate as if this were the case. Formal designations of property ownership imply that ownership on paper is the same as control in practice, when in fact the effective control over forest resources may depart dramatically from what the official documents and laws say.[2] Finally, it gives the false impression that there are clear differences among state, communal, and private property.

In fact, when the specific rights related to forest resources are separated out, it becomes obvious that in most cases rights are already split among government, community, and individuals.[3] These rights include *direct* rights to:

- develop forest resources (for example, planting trees, establishing tourist facilities)
- extract forest resources
- sell the outputs
- sell the rights to engage in the above activities
- share in the income produced by forest uses

Societies also have to decide who should provide these assurances and how they should be provided. In addition to the obvious issue of who gets access to the forest resources, there is a more complex question of who ought to have the authority to decide who gets access. Therefore the range of rights also includes the rights to *control* forest uses:

- decide what forest resources will be developed
- decide on the rates of extraction
- decide on who should be allowed to extract
- decide on the markets and prices for outputs
- decide on whether resource rights can be sold and the conditions of sale

These specific user rights are divided in complicated ways in any given situation, making the usual distinctions of private, common, and state property of little use. The situation of a private user (individual, family, or company) holding all of these control rights as well as the rights to engage directly in forest use is rather rare. More typically, individual users are limited in their rights to use resources even though they are legally "owned" by the individual. When the control rights are in the hands of others, whether the government or the community, the individual's direct rights are effectively limited. The most striking example of this is in South Korea, where the Forest Development Law of 1970 empowered county governments to require certain landowners to devote their private land to forest plantations. If the private owner failed to comply, then the government could authorize the local village forestry association to undertake the operation on a cost-sharing basis with the private owner (Gregersen 1988: 227–29).

As for what seems to be community ownership, much of the exploitation and profit-taking is actually done privately. To be sure, there are truly communal activities, such as village tree planting, teams of *xate* or Brazil nut gatherers, or cooperatives to process and sell pine resin. But very often "communal" forests are exploited by individual community members who cut and sell trees, tap rubber, or extract any of a wide range of products from communal property for personal gain as they might from private land; the difference is that the community holds the control rights. This is because even on communal property the community often assigns private uses of particular resource sites and restricts certain uses or the rate of use, but does not literally exploit the resources collectively. The community may or may not require the individual extractors to contribute some of their gains to other community members or to the community's central treasury.

For example, according to customary practice in Lesotho, cleared land in or close to the village is assigned by the village chief to adult males, whose families devote the land to agriculture, orchards, or residence. Upon the death of that male, the property reverts back to the chief for reassignment. Natural forestland, in contrast, is managed by the village, which permits the private collection of fallen wood but allows private chopping only with the permission of the chief (Turner 1988: 199–203).

As for forests formally under state or government control, the differences between effective government use rights and the rights of individuals and communities get blurred when governments lease land or grant extraction concessions to companies, individuals, or communities. In these cases, the government essentially regulates the private or communal use of forest resources; much of the benefits go to the users (whether logging firms or largely poor traditional farmers), shared with the government to the degree that the government charges for the wood and nontimber products removed from state lands. In other cases, state-owned forestland is simply left to others to exploit, without any official granting of rights. In either situation, private and communal forest use occurs on government-owned forestland. The government reserves the control rights, though it often does not exercise them.

Another blurring of government and community comes when the community is defined as everyone within a given geographical area. "Communal" (or "community") property is not simply accessible or usable by members of a community; its uses are also controlled or governed by bodies made up of members of the community. Ignoring this fact is what led earlier assessments of communal property to assume that it would be used without control or discipline by community members. [4] So communal property is also subject to governance, and when the community is the whole set of local inhabitants, this governance is equivalent to local government. For example, in India, Nepal, and other South Asian countries, village or multivillage councils called *panchayats* often control various plots of land. The *panchayat* in a certain sense represents the community, yet it is also a form of government and (especially in the eyes of the national and state governments) a level of government within the wider framework from the national level on down.[5]

In contrast, when "community" refers to a group within the larger population of all residents of a given area, there is an important difference between community governance and local government. This has important consequences for the issue of excluding some potential forest users in order to make forest development and responsible exploitation profitable for those who do qualify. However, the leadership of the geographical community is often not at all the same as the multiple leaderships of the communities of interest and identification that exist within the geographical area.

Risks Facing Private, State, and Community Forestry Management

Risk of others' access.

The risk of unstable user rights can arise for two reasons: those with the control rights to determine access may reassign direct user rights from the original user to other users, and those with control rights may neglect or lose their capacity to enforce exclusion, leaving the forest in an open-access condition. The possibility of reassignment of user rights makes state control risky for people who are operating under leases or temporary privileges provided by the government. What the government gives, it can take away. Especially when one government is replaced by another, the forest users face the risk that their arrangements with the state will fall apart. The traditional forest users also face this risk when newcomers succeed in getting government recognition of *their* user rights. Until quite recently most logging concession agreements between governments and commercial companies give the companies exclusive rights to extract forest products. Local people were seen as encroachers, were denounced as the major culprits in deforestation, and came under increasingly harsh treatment by the forestry departments under pressure from the commercial loggers.[6]

Governments frequently recognize the user rights of colonizers over the rights of long-standing residents. Forestlands are a convenient safety valve for population pressures from densely settled areas. Forests appear to be lush, fertile areas even though their agricultural productivity is often very limited. The allure of moving into apparently fertile forested areas is therefore very appealing for landless people, for ranchers waiting for colonizers to clear and then abandon the land, and to governments searching for an easy to deal with overpopulation.

The open-access situation arises when government claims control over forestland that it cannot, or will not, regulate. The traditional users lose their authority to exclude encroachers, unless they wish to take up arms in defiance of laws that place the policing power in the hands of the government. This has happened in Honduras, where farmers extend their fences to include forestland that is legally part of the national forests (Jones 1988: 156); in the Brazilian Amazon, where the greatest source of deforestation has been clearing destined for cattle ranches (Browder 1988: 251); and in numerous countries where illegal commercial logging, slash-and-burn agriculture by recent settlers, and fuelwood removal goes on out of sight of government forestry guards.

User rights are clearly most secure when the control rights are held by communities, defined according to traditional user groups. Traditional user communities have a strong incentive to keep outsiders from gaining access to the forest resource. Community resource managers have little incentive to strip away one community member's share to enrich the others. The community members making these decisions have to live with all of the members of the community; denying community members their fair share of benefits would risk angering friends, neighbors, and relatives. Unfair treatment would also undermine the reputation and acceptability of the community resource managers and might even provide an excuse for the government (which is generally not very sensitive to the fallout of disappointing traditional forest users) to intervene.

In contrast, when the "community" is defined as the whole set of people within a geographical area, resource management is essentially in the hands of the local government, or at the least in the hands of whoever has the most political power to gain control over the resource management institutions. In the South Asian cases mentioned previously, for example, where the village councils called *panchayats* often hold the control rights on behalf of the entire village, individual opportunities to use the forest are frequently assigned to the friends and relatives of the wealthier village members who sit on the councils. The traditional forest users may face a big risk because they are socially and economically different from the leaders who dominate the local government or the specific resource management institutions.

The security of individual user rights in a situation of private control rights as well as direct user rights depends on how stable the situation is and how prepared other institutions are to defend private rights if they are challenged. As long as private titles are clear and recognized by everyone, privately held control rights and direct user rights reduce the forest user's risks of losing profitable access. The problem, of course, is that titles to forestlands and specific forest uses are rarely clear; in many cases they do not even exist as legal documents. As the agricultural frontier moves into forested areas, the willingness of outsiders to accept established entitlements is also doubtful. In these circumstances, the lack of community control rights means that the defense of private direct user rights falls to the government. In effect the government, in deciding on whether to defend the direct rights of specific users, takes over the control rights. Therefore, where there is uncertainty or challenges to private user rights, the traditional forest user also faces the same risk arising from government control.

Risk of stricter regulation.

The threat that profitability will be eaten away by stricter government regulation, even if the forest user retains access, arises whenever the government has the discretion to tighten the rules of resource use on state land that is leased or allowed to be used by others, or to impose stricter regulations on nongovernment land. In other words, the risk arises if the government claims direct user rights, but also if the government claims the control rights over what forest resources will be developed, the rates of extraction, and the markets and prices for outputs. In many countries, for example, the government has imposed a limit on the minimum width of trees that can be harvested. This obviously results in lower immediate profits for the resource extractor.

When the control rights are held by the traditional user community, the chances that community resource managers will impose unprofitable restrictions on extraction are reduced because these community leaders themselves rely on the resources for their own incomes. Furthermore, giving themselves unfair advantages through more lenient regulations on their own forest uses would be costly for the community leaders for the same reasons that denying access to fellow community members would be costly.

Again we see a contrast between this situation of the traditional forest user community and the entire geographical community. If the village or district controls the forest use, but the local leaders do not themselves depend on the use, these leaders do not bear the costs of unduly harsh restrictions. For example, many areas of cultivation and residence are near forested hills that may be subject to modest, small-scale logging by traditional forest users. It would be easy for the village or district council to forbid all tree cutting in the area, as long as the user community that traditionally removed trees is not a powerful group within the village or district. The view of the leadership may be that no cutting is better than modest cutting. Yet in the long run, the restriction on logging will discourage replanting and may well provoke larger-scale, illegal cutting.

The risk for the forest user holding purer property rights allowing unregulated extraction is that some level of government will decide to change the rules. Even if the private resource user is mindful of the long-term profitability of his or her resource use, the concern over spillover effects, or the simple desire to have more control, may prompt government intervention. Without a community organization overseeing responsible uses, the government may well see a vacuum to fill.

Risk of exclusion by nongovernmental "owners."

When the government leases state-controlled forests to particular users, or recognizes the rights of specific users on nongovernment land, these users often try to keep other users away from their resources, even if these other users have had direct user rights. Often, when the government grants leases to commercial loggers, the loggers declare the land off-limits to the traditional forest users. Sometimes, especially when governments promise to provide greater financial resources to develop a forest, outsiders rush to establish property claims where no formal or clear property titles exist.

Risk of a low share of the community's forestry earnings.

Where forest use rights are held communally, there is a risk that a particular community member will receive an inadequate share of the income. This can arise in several ways. The resource managers may simply deny a fair share to a community member who worked hard in forest development or extraction. Corruption may be the cause, or disputes over the basis for sharing. In either case, the community's organizational structure (for example, careful monitoring to make sure that embezzlement does not occur and mechanisms to resolve disputes fairly and peacefully) is very important and is discussed at length in Chapter 4.

Yet while any type of community organization can fall prey to corruption and disputes over how to distribute the earnings, here too we see that communities of identification and interest, as opposed to communities defined by geographical boundaries, are likely to do better in terms of this risk. The social costs to the decision maker of being unfair are very high within the traditional community. In addition, disputes within groups of identification are typically more likely to be resolved fairly and peacefully because of the closer social ties within such communities, the existence of traditional ways of resolving differences, and the narrower differences in wealth and power within these communities.

A surprising risk of receiving an inadequate share arises when the government tries to privatize user rights in what had been a communal user-right arrangement. In many such arrangements, the community has an obligation to assist widows, orphans, and the elderly without children who can work on the farms and in the forests. If the government comes in and offers to grant formal property rights to individuals who are currently working the forests, it may well exclude community members not in a position to exploit the resources at that time. The traditional community may have rules that recognize the history of contributions of families that are not currently in a position to work actively, but the government is less likely to be sensitive to these historically based obligations. This is a strong rationale for the community, rather than the government, to be responsible for assigning direct user rights to individuals and families.

Risk of inadequate credit.

Credit, important both to finance forest resource development and to provide emergency income before forest products can be harvested, depends on three essential things, all in the eyes of the lender: the capacity of the borrower to earn enough income to pay the interest and repay the principal, the willingness of the borrower to meet these obligations, and the existence of valuable resources (collateral) that the lender could successfully claim if the borrower fails to meet the obligations.

When the government (or its state agencies) directly manages state-owned forest resources, the issue of lending arises if the budget of the managing agency requires resources controlled by another. In many countries, the forestry agencies are indeed underfunded, but the issue is more the desire of the central government to fund forest development than it is a matter of creditworthiness. The more important credit issue arises when the government leases state-owned land for private or communal exploitation. Since the exploiters cannot claim ownership of the land, the land (and the user rights) can hardly serve as collateral. They often have to depend on government credit, which has its own risks. For one thing, it is often distributed according to political considerations. Government credit is typically at interest rates below the market rates, because when governments offer credit they generally do so to gain political support. Therefore the interest payments do not replenish the loan fund, while demand for cheap credit remains high. In this situation of scarce credit, people with closer connections to the officials making the loans are more likely to get them. Low-income forest users rarely qualify. For another thing, the government may be inconsistent in its willingness to continue to lend.

In the case of communal forest resources, the community's access to credit depends on its ability to make credible commitments and to be able to offer some of its assets as collateral. The risk therefore is that the community cannot find the internal unity to agree to make binding commitments, or that its assets cannot be accepted as collateral.

One of the most frequently cited cases of the economic drawbacks of communal property is the Mexican *ejido*, the twentieth century version of a communal property arrangement dating back from before the Spanish conquest. In the 1910s, the *ejido* arrangement was reestablished as part of Mexico's vast land reform, to protect (by constitutional article) land redistributed to communities from being lost by that community. The typical *ejido* arrangement—a very good example of mixed private and communal user rights—grants individual families the rights to use parcels of *ejido* land and to pass these rights on to their offspring. If a family lacks people to work the land, it would revert to the *ejido* community.

Yet there are important variants. For example, in the Chunhuhub *ejido* in the Mexican state of Quintana Roo, each head of household requests from the *ejido* council a particular area of land for farming; the eventual allocation is determined in a community meeting. Crops are grown for a few seasons, and then the area is left fallow, reverting back to the authority of the *ejido* council. In fallow areas, the *ejido* families are allowed to extract whatever resources they need. However, if they wish to take plants or to fell timber for commercial sale, they must get permission from the *ejido* council or win approval in a community meeting (Anderson 1992).

Regardless of the internal governance of the *ejido*, according to Mexico's constitution and law, the *ejido* could not rent, sell, or give away the land that it "owned." Until the 1990s, the widely recognized problem with *ejidos* was that because they could not sell land or put it up as collateral for loans, many *ejidos* failed to obtain outside financing for agricultural development, let alone for forest development and harvesting projects. *Ejido* communities have shown a general lack of enthusiasm to plant trees or to maintain forest resources. Afforestation, with very little financial return for many years, has not been an attractive option for devoting scarce resources.

In reaction to the low productivity of *ejidos,* [7] the Mexican government began various efforts in the early 1990s to privatize them. The new policy is to allow individual *ejido* members to sell their assigned land, thus allowing the land to be put up as collateral, as well as allowing the sellers to get income before a given stand of forest is ready to harvest. The government's implicit diagnosis was that the communal nature of the property was the problem; the solution trades communal management and sharing for better financial conditions.

Yet the real obstacle to the sale of *ejido* land, and to its use as collateral, was not the community but rather the government policy that limited the communities' rights to sell or otherwise "lose" the land. The *ejido* arrangement is not truly a pure case of common property, because the community members have not held all of the rights associated with full property ownership. Expressed in terms of the various user rights, the *ejido* arrangement gave the community the direct rights to develop, extract, sell, and share the income from forest resources, but not to sell the resource use rights. It gave the community the control rights over development and exploitation, and to decide which individuals and families could be involved, within the broad limits established by the state that only *ejido* members could qualify for involvement. The state, furthermore, held the control rights to decide who could sell the direct user rights—and until recently decided that no one could.

There is a clear alternative to privatizing the *ejido*: the Mexican government can simply recognize the *ejido's* right to sell its own land, its user rights, or both.

Private forest users with land ownership or user rights that can be legally transferred have a form of collateral, but low-income forest users may not have sufficiently great loan needs to attract the lenders, who are generally much more interested in lending large sums than small, or sufficiently valuable land or user rights to warrant the loan. The risk of the small-scale, private forest user is in his or her isolation. The availability of government credit to the individual forest user, as mentioned previously, is also limited.

Of course, even if collateral is available, there is a risk that credit will not be. This issue is taken up in the next chapter.

Risk of cash shortage.

When forest users have or anticipate cash needs before the appropriate time to harvest their forest resources, the two relevant options are borrowing and selling. The same problems of credit arise for borrowing for emergency cash needs as arise for borrowing to finance forest development. Therefore the isolation of individual forest users is the source of private users' borrowing risk; users who lease state-owned forestland generally lack collateral. Communities can offset this risk by pooling their property or rights as long as government policy does not block using communal property or rights as collateral.

Selling forest assets before the forest products are harvestable faces two difficulties. First, as in the case of the *ejido* property discussed above, the government may not permit such sales. In terms of rights, selling forest assets is possible for both private owners and communities, if the private or communal forest users have the control rights as well as the direct use rights. In other words, private and communal forest users have the sale option as long as the constitution, laws, and government do not forbid these sales. Our argument, again, is that problems only arise when government retains the control rights; this is not a true problem of communal rights. Second, customers may not be available to buy forested property or future harvesting rights. This requires a market for land and forest resources, a topic discussed in the next chapter.

Risk of low market prices.

The risk of declining prices of forest products can affect users of all types; the question is whether different arrangements of user rights can reduce the likelihood that government actions or other conditions will drag down prices. Three conditions frequently result in unusually low prices: world market declines for exported items such as rubber, Brazil nuts, or timber; government actions; and low prices offered by middlemen.

In the face of declines in the international prices of wood products, the government is often more disposed to help out state agencies involved in wood-products export than private or communal exploiters, in order to protect the jobs of the workers employed by the state agencies. However, if this means that forest exploitation needs to be subsidized in order to be profitable, it is an unwise practice, because the forest is being exploited without sufficient economic justification for the society as a whole.

When the community holds the full set of forest user rights (including the control rights over deciding on the rate of resource exploitation), it can decide how much to exploit in times of low prices. Large enough communities can often can ride out the period of lower prices by pooling their resources to protect community members with the greatest needs for emergency cash.

When the government holds the rights to establish the sale prices (that is, it chooses to go against the free market for forest products), the most common problem is government-imposed ceilings on forest products, especially raw timber. The government may require the output to be sold to state agencies, as in the case of Honduras, or otherwise reduce the incomes that the resource users can gain from the forest. Many governments, for example, have banned the export of logs. The stated reason is usually that the country would do better economically if more finished wood products, such as lumber, plywood, and furniture, were manufactured within the country. Whatever the validity of this argument—which has been repeatedly challenged—the outcome for the loggers, whether small-scale or large, is to reduce the price of timber because the export market is cut off.

To reduce this serious risk, community organizations may have greater success than isolated individuals. Government price setting is often part of the political process, in that the decisions reflect the balance of pressures from the forest users and the consumers of forest products. The better organized the forest users, the more likely that they can pressure the government to eliminate price ceilings or at least to avoid setting prices of forest products too low to permit the forest users from making reasonable profits.

The final price risk, discussed at greater length in Chapter 4, is that middlemen will buy cheaply from the forest users and reap the profits themselves. While the profiteering of middlemen is often exaggerated, when it does occur, the right and capacity of the forest exploiter to take on some of these middleman activities (such as processing, transporting, and marketing processed wood products) become important. In such cases, the private, small-scale forest user again faces the greatest risk, simply by virtue of limited resources, whereas the community can often pool its resources to move into these activities (as in the cases of Honduran resin tappers reviewed in Chapter 4).

Risk of harmful spillover effects.

Governments often retain the control rights because they fear not just that forest users will harm their own future chances, but that their irresponsible actions will harm the incomes or well-being of other people. These harmful spillover effects [8] are the biggest challenge to community control rights, because communities often do engage in forest exploitation that causes damage to other individuals or communities. Communities of common interest and identification may well cause consequences that affect people beyond that community. Some steps can be taken to link up communities so that they will have to take account of damage by one to another. For example, as community groups join with one another to become more powerful in relating to the government and other groups, their expanded geographical scope makes less of their impacts external to the members of the greater community. Even so, some effects will remain external. Even the widest association of community logging cooperatives has no particular incentive to worry about soil erosion on lands used beyond its own members' control.

Therefore this is the one risk best addressed through

governance by the geographically defined community, since all residents are affected. The guiding principle is for the boundaries of the governing community to be roughly equivalent to the boundaries of the harmful effects, so that there is no incentive to allow harmful effects to go unaddressed. Local, district, and provincial (or state) governments may be relevant, depending on the scope of the potential environmental or resource damage. Lower levels of government, as long as they cover affected areas, are likely to be more responsive to environmental effects than are more distant, higher-level governments.

Yet the authority of the government to regulate forest uses for the sake of environmental protection also carries responsibilities. Because these responsibilities are not always met, the formal control rights do not eliminate the risk that the damage will occur. Another aspect of the Mexican experience in the state of Quintana Roo demonstrates this point. In granting forest concessions to a commercial logging company MIQRO, the state government had the obligation to enforce harvesting and replanting regulations, as well as to require the logging company to allow access to the forest by local people for traditional uses. Yet Maderas Industrializados de Quintana Roo (MIQRO) and the small-scale contractors excluded local people and neglected reforestation (Bray et al. 1993), as the company essentially ignored the terms of its contract. The government was either unwilling or unable to enforce those terms, and the local community lost out as a result.

Conclusions

This chapter has demonstrated why assurance of future, profitable forest use is important. First, there is a clear relationship between assurance of future use and willingness to exploit the resource at a reasonable pace. Assurance of future use is also clearly linked to willingness to exploit the resource responsibly rather than wastefully. Second, when people know that they will retain the right to exploit a resource, or to sell their right to exploit the resource, they will be more willing to invest in developing the resource. Third, clear indications of who can use particular resources will often signal to others that encroaching on current users would not succeed.

Essentially, leaving resource management to the local area council leads to a serious "flattening" of the otherwise rich, complex diversity of many communities of interest and identification. Community user rights should not mean that one institution speaks for everyone within the geographical area. If the user rights of the *various* user communities within a geographical area have some authority, then resource use patterns will emerge from a broader process of participation by these groups. To be sure, sometimes these interactions result in confrontations and even physical conflict, but they are less likely to result in the wealthier, more powerful residents of the area wresting the benefits of resource extraction away from the poorer traditional resource users.

3   Overcoming Economic
           Obstacles in Forestry

Sustainable forestry requires that forest users view forest resource development as an attractive business proposition and
judge overly rapid, wasteful, immediate exploitation as run-
ning against their own economic interests. This chapter
focuses in more depth on the economic risks, introduced in
Chapter 2, that threaten the economic attractiveness of forest
development or make immediate overextraction seem like the
best economic option. While Chapter 2 dealt with how different rights arrangements address these risks, this chapter explores a much broader range of instruments and strategies for
communities and governments to make forest development
and exploitation securely profitable. Without this secure profitability, responsible forest use is far less likely. Of course,
many forest users already rely on some of these strategies. Yet
it is still useful to lay out the whole range of strategies
as a checklist so that community organizations and governments can consider whether they have overlooked promising
alternatives.

Two related arguments emerge from our survey of economic risks and the strategies to overcome them. First, we will
argue that community organization of forest activities is crucial for overcoming many of these economic difficulties. While
many of the specific instruments seem to be technical, organized community action is often necessary to identify, undertake, and finance them. Second, we will argue that
governments can help forest users to secure their forestry incomes without price controls, subsidized credit, direct control

of forests, or other heavy-handed interventions. Indeed, strong government intervention in forestry creates even greater insecurities.

Types of Economic Risks

To understand the economic issues involved in forest uses, it is important to understand the logic of investment. People who are planning to invest their time, effort, money, or land all go through a similar thought process, whether they are deciding to finance an office building in New York or to plant a woodlot in a Ugandan village. The broad question is whether the expected income (in the form of cash or products) from the investment will best serve their needs over the life of the investment, compared to alternative investment opportunities.

The life of the investment generally begins with an initial phase of rather high expenses but little income from the project (for example, constructing the building before anyone pays rent; caring for the trees before they are large enough to harvest). For some types of investments, this crucial initial period is relatively short—planting annual crops like corn or potatoes yields income sooner than do trees. Early income is worth more to the investor than later income and may be less risky as well.

The second phase involves the mature operation of the project, during which incomes are usually highest and the major costs are for operational inputs (for example, labor, electricity, raw materials) and maintenance. Often the most crucial factor here is the price of the project's output; many economic disasters result from conditions, often imposed by the government, that keep the output prices from reaching the levels they would achieve in a market in which buyers and sellers are free to negotiate the price. An important option considered by investors is whether selling the asset during this stage, or even during the first stage, would be advantageous. There is sometimes a third phase, in which the project fades or is terminated because of declining incomes. For some investments, including forests, this third phase can be avoided, but only with proper maintenance and disciplined use.

Deciding on whether to invest in forest development requires three steps:

1. anticipating the income and the costs of forestry activities compared to available alternatives
2. weighing the value of income likely to come in earlier versus later years
3. deciding how much importance to give to avoiding riskier investments even if their most likely incomes are higher than other alternatives

The challenge of encouraging small-scale development and exploitation of forests lies in the contrast between the long-term and relatively risky nature of many forestry ventures aiming at sustainability and the often short-term, risk-avoiding nature of many of the people necessary for these ventures to succeed. Low-income forest users are often forced by economic necessity to have strong preferences for early income and to engage in low-risk activities. However, we will see that the risks and even the time frame of forestry development can be reduced. In this and later chapters, we will also see that some government policies have actually reduced expected forestry income, cut off opportunities for early earnings, and increased various types of risks. This is certainly discouraging in terms of the prospects of relying on government. But it is encouraging in terms of the potential to bring sustainable forestry initiatives more in line with the economic interests of small-scale forest users, through both policy reform and greater reliance on community organization. We even find important roles for constructive government action.

Economic implications of physical risks.

Nature is not evenhanded when forest developments turn out differently from what was planned: there is a greater chance that surprising outcomes will result in lower yields, and therefore lower incomes, than that these will be pleasant surprises of higher yields and profits. Forest development depends on whole series of necessary physical steps (for example, seeds successfully germinating; trees converting soil nutrients, sunlight, and water into adequate growth; trees being pollinated and distributing their seeds at the right time). These steps can be disrupted by a host of unknowable future events: fires, insect infestations, too little or too much rain, disappearance of animals contributing to pollination or seed germination, etc. Other physical disruptions involve the actions of other human beings, who may cut or burn the forest, remove crucial animals, poison the soils with mining chemicals, etc. It is most unlikely that unanticipated events or conditions will lead to better outcomes from the delicate chains of steps required to grow trees and other forest resources.

Short time horizons.

People's needs naturally vary. Some people need income right away; this is often the case with very low-income people. Some people, even if they are not desperate for income at one point in time, may have emergency cash needs that require them to try to liquidate their investments. This is clearly more likely to occur for people with low savings. Therefore the weighing of income that comes in earlier rather than later years will be different for different people. *Low-income forest users typically have to put great value in income that can be earned, or at least can be available if needed, in the early years.* In other words, low-income forest users are often unable to afford long time horizons. The obvious problem is that the physical growth even of fast-growing trees requires five to ten years, if not more, to yield significant incomes. The vicious cycle that emerges is that governments respond to the desperate actions of the poor by excluding them even more from the forests, thereby reducing their income-earning opportunities even further.

Coping with uncertainty.

The uncertainties in choosing these investments come from three sources. First, people do not really know what their future needs will be. They may have huge medical bills later in the year; their crops might fail; they may have to pay a dowry. Second, people do not really know whether the planned investment will be successful *physically*. Crops fail; trees are damaged by fire or insects; buildings collapse during construction. Third, people cannot predict with certainty that the project will be successful *financially*. Prices drop; costs increase; markets may be cut off.

These uncertainties loom very large for low-income forest users, who cannot afford economic disappointments. It is true that tolerating risk is often the only way to gain big returns, because safe investments tend to attract more people so that the competition reduces the chances of high profits. However, low-income people who resort to small-scale forestry cannot afford to be big gamblers. Their willingness to sink resources into forest development, as well as to forgo immediate opportunities to overharvest forest resources that they did not develop, depends on bringing these uncertainties within reasonable limits.

Therefore the means for creating the willingness to invest in forest development are:

1. reducing physical risks
2. reducing market risks
3. reducing the uncertainties concerning physical and economic risks as much as possible, so that forest users can make more reasonable decisions on how to cope with them
4. bringing the opportunities for income earning closer to the present *if needed*
5. reducing the general economic insecurity of forest users so that they will not shrink from making long-term investments in forest development

Reducing the Physical Risks of Specific Forestry Ventures

The physical risks of specific forestry ventures include natural disasters; inappropriate or excessive exploitation by others, whether inside or outside of the user group; damage to the forest resource due to other activities; and exclusion by the government or others claiming ownership.

Physical risks from natural disasters can be limited in

their impact, if not completely eliminated, by the twin strategies of physical separation and variety. Separate plots can keep pests and diseases from spreading, and different locations can reduce the risk that soil or water problems will affect the entire planting. It has been increasingly recognized that single-species plantations face larger risks of devastation by pests, diseases, weather, or lack of nutrients than do plantations of mixed tree species (Kanowski and Savill 1992).

Technology can also have a major role in reducing physical risks, from discoveries of how to inoculate trees with microorganisms for ensuring better growth, to genetic breeding of trees and other plants to be more resistant to pests and diseases (Kanowski and Savill 1992: 376–77). However, technologies impose their own requirements and costs. They have to be identified—and often paid for. Technologies usually pose training challenges, and they may involve their own risks if they are untried or inappropriate for that specific application. Individuals, especially if they are very poor, are often slow to adopt new technologies. Therefore collective action, with its potential to pool resources and shield individuals from risk, can play an important part in getting technologies to be accepted. Governments can play a complementary role in financing the development of technologies and providing technical assistance.

The physical risks involving encroachments by other forest exploiters must be addressed through strong community organizations (as outlined in Chapter 4). Group strength is needed to negotiate with others and to stand up to them physically if necessary. Clear group and territorial boundaries from the outset obviously help. Yet since user groups have limited policing or legal powers regarding the actions of others, government has another potential role in upholding boundaries (elaborated in Chapter 5).

The physical damage caused by the spillover effects of others' actions poses much the same challenge as do encroachments: intergroup relations, rather than technological fixes, are crucial. Community organizations must decide whether to negotiate with those responsible for the damage, take physical actions to reduce spillover effects, appeal to the government to regulate damaging effects, or some combination of these options. The government has to decide how to respond to such appeals, and how strictly to regulate in order to prevent spill-over effects from occurring (see Chapter 5).

Reducing Market Risks

The profitability of business operations depends on the difference between costs, reflecting the prices of inputs; and sales, reflecting the prices of outputs. Sometimes forest users, particularly if they are operating on land controlled by others, have to pay royalties that are not only high, but are also inflexible regardless of the profits or losses from forestry uses. This leaves the forest user to bear all of the risk if revenues are disappointing. Because government officials have to observe rates established by laws and regulations, it is often the charges for using state lands for forestry that are least flexible. For example, the pine resin tappers of Honduras have had to pay a nearly constant fee of US$10 per quarter metric ton of resin to the state forestry corporation, local government, and their cooperatives, even though the market price for pine resin during the 1980s fell to US$16 after reaching a high of over US$40 (Stanley 1991: 31). Yet fixed fees can also occur on private lands. In Brazil, the rubber tappers who work the trees controlled by large-scale "rubber barons" pay sizable rents that (along with the practical necessity of buying their supplies from the landlords) often keep them in indefinite debt (Allegretti 1990: 253).

More frequently, though, those with forest user rights can harvest without having to make significant payments for access. Their input costs are rather stable and known: their own labor, hired labor, tools, and (in forest development) seedlings, possibly vehicles, etc. The major economic risk, therefore, is in the output prices. Part of this risk is pure market risk. Timber prices are volatile, for example, as recessions in industrial countries reduce the demand for lumber, and the major expansion of timber exports by one country may have an effect on the world market price of timber for all. Brazil nuts, rubber, and other nontimber products face the likelihood of declining prices because of expansions in production and substitutions of other products.

However, so-called market risks are often heavily influenced by, or even caused by, government policy. As mentioned in Chapter 2, governments often introduce price risk by imposing price controls or restricting markets. Price ceilings on raw materials from the countryside are often singled out as the major reason for rural poverty and stagnation. More subtle price distortions are introduced through policies that restrict the market. In many countries, governments have banned the export of raw logs, leaving the timber producers only the domestic market for their sales. Governments also frequently grant export licenses to only a handful of forest-product exporters, who can organize into cartels to gain advantage in buying from many, often unorganized, raw-material suppliers.

Therefore forest users have two tacks for reducing market risks. One is political: to press the government to recognize that the right to sell a product at the market price is a crucial part of the user rights package. Fortunately, governments all over the world have become increasingly aware of the importance of market-sensitive prices for economic efficiency. Yet governments, particularly when their own budgets rely on buying or selling forest products, have been slow to apply market principles to forestry. Undoubtedly the pressure that forest users can exert on government to eliminate government restrictions on forest-product prices is stronger to the degree that the users can organize.

The other tack is to accommodate the remaining risk of disappointing markets and prices through business strategies. The two most relevant strategies are risk sharing and diversification.

Risk Sharing.

Forestry ventures, like other business ventures, require a combination of contributions of money, labor, and natural resources. Whoever provides one or more of these contributions, and stands to lose it if the forestry venture is not successful, bears some of the risk. Viewed this way, every community forestry initiative is already a risk-sharing arrangement. That is, the risk of any single venture can be spread among many forest users, each with a contribution that would not be a financial disaster if the venture fails.

Joint ventures. Yet the forest-user community can reduce its risks further by arranging for contributions from people or institutions outside of the community. These *joint ventures* may involve government, state enterprises, nongovernmental organizations (NGOs), private companies, forest-product processors, etc. Many paper companies and large-scale sawmills have been willing to provide seedlings, tools, and even their land to individuals and cooperatives in profit-sharing ventures. The relatively enlightened social forestry programs in the Indian state of Gujarat have also recognized the importance of forestry partnerships by offering joint ventures with the poorest villages, which have only their labor to contribute. For strip plantations along roads, canals, and railroad tracks, the government buys the seeds and pays for the technical assistance; the villages split the earnings with the Gujarat Forestry Department on a pre-established proportional basis (Dalvi and Shukla 1988: 44-45). As documented in Chapter 5, these programs have to be carefully targeted to the groups with established user rights, or else the inflow of government financing may attract outsiders seeking easy gains.

Crop insurance. Efforts to set up insurance funds covering agricultural crops have been rather common; among them are efforts to insure trees. These efforts have been attempted both by governments and by community organizations. Insurance often seems like an obvious response to risk. Over the course of the years needed for trees to grow to commercial size, there will typically be several occurrences that could be considered as insurable, physical risks to the trees: drought or floods, fire, pest infestations, etc. Insurance is a direct form of risk spreading, as the insurance fund allows the costs of an insured disaster to be borne by other insured people who have contributed to the fund, or by other sources (such as the government) willing to subsidize the insurance fund.

Yet crop insurance programs in general face severe problems, both in developed and developing countries. [1] The first problem is that insured tree growers have less incentive to care for their trees when the insurance is there to save them from risky actions or neglect. Sometimes collecting the insurance may be more attractive than continuing with tree growing (for example, if timber or other tree-products prices are expected to go down).

Crop insurance requires high administrative costs in order to prevent cheating. The government that tries to establish a crop insurance system therefore faces the choices of charging very high premiums to cover the administrative costs, providing government subsidies to accomplish this, or simply not trying to prevent and discover cheating.

When disasters strike one farmer or tree-grower's crops, they are likely to affect many farmers or tree-growers, and the insurance fund will be quickly depleted. Generally the institutions responsible for providing the insurance fund are not very diversified. Therefore, a widespread condition, such as drought or fire, affecting many tree-growers may well bankrupt the insurance fund.

Another problem is that often the best tree-growers have developed their own strategies for reducing risk (for example, diversifying their crops, planting in several different physical locations, etc.), and therefore they are not interested in paying premiums for insurance. The result is, first, that the insurance fund that does not include these people ends up insuring the less competent tree-growers, who naturally have the highest risk. Second, if the government insurance fund requires that all tree-growers participate, the resentment against being forced to pay premiums may often lead the tree-growers to try to take advantage of the system through cheating and even deliberate destruction of their own trees in order to collect the insurance.

In addition, if the insurance program is to be self-financing, the premiums have to be high to reflect the true costs. In this situation, only the rich could afford to pay for crop insurance and the ones who are in greatest need of risk-sharing strategies—the poor—will be excluded.

The limited successes with crop insurance have been found

in community-managed mutual insurance funds, in which the members decide collectively who can belong. This reduces the danger that farmers with poor records will participate. Because the mutual fund members usually live close to one another, and are often tied by family connections, there is also less risk of cheating or other irresponsible behavior.

A very different concept of insurance is to safeguard the incomes of tree-growers by guaranteeing minimum prices for the trees and nontimber products. This would typically require government involvement, because few other institutions would have the resources to pay higher prices. If the government makes sales to the government institution optional, rather than required as under the marketing board arrangement, such a scheme could help the tree-growers. Yet, as a thinly-disguised form of subsidy, it too runs the strong risk to the government that when timber prices are low, the fund will be bankrupted.

Merchant middlemen. Reliance on merchant middlemen[2] who purchase and resell (or process) forest products is another important risk-reducing device—which may be surprising considering all the criticism of the middleman role. There are many middleman arrangements, varying in terms of whether the middleman advances credit to the original sellers or the buyers, offers a fixed or varying price to the seller, becomes involved in processing and further steps of marketing the product, and so on. The usefulness of middlemen, besides their ability to get the product to market and sometimes their capacity to provide credit, is in their willingness to absorb some of the risk of falling prices. In Honduras, for example, the resin-processing cartel provides a fixed price over the six-month tapping season, even if the refined resin price falls during that period (Stanley 1991: 31).

So why are merchant middlemen so reviled? The typical attitude is reflected in the view of Fernandes, Menon, and Viegas (1988: 131), referring to the Indian state of Orissa:

The relationship between the forest dwellers and the middlemen is symbolic of the position in which the weaker

61

sections find themselves. They do not have any bargaining power and are at the mercy of the middlemen who exploit them in various forms.

These critics argue that middlemen who purchase firewood and minor forest products from low-income forest users offer them low prices, lend them money in lean months in order to exact lower prices during the harvesting months, and cheat them when measuring their produce. When cheating occurs, it is certainly unjustifiable and ought to be addressed by community efforts to monitor the measuring process. Yet the issues of low prices and middleman lending require reconsideration. Aside from cheating, private market prices are dictated by supply, demand, and competition, not by the evil intentions of particular people in the process. In any event, the existence of competition among middlemen will raise the prices that they will be willing to offer—a matter that community organizations can address by creating alternative marketing channels. The criticism that merchant middlemen lend to forest users during lean periods is a peculiar one indeed, in light of the advantages of obtaining credit. The essential point is that middlemen take on this risk in exchange for the opportunity to make large profits when the prices they can get for resold or processed products are high. To criticize middlemen for making big profits when prices boom is to ignore the losses they may take when prices collapse.

Government marketing boards.   What of the possibility of government institutions serving as middlemen? Government marketing boards and state enterprises have operated in many countries, usually defended precisely on the grounds that they can stabilize the prices obtained by primary producers to insulate these producers from the damage of low prices. However, it has been shown time and time again that state marketing boards are managed by officials who want to increase the take of the board itself, or get captured by government policy makers who want to increase the government's revenues; in either case the strategy becomes to offer very low prices to producers (Bates 1988). This would be little different from the profit motive that the private middlemen have, except that these government agencies often have the power to force the producers to sell to the marketing board or not at all. Therefore the marketing boards can and often do impose prices that are lower than what the private market would provide. Evidence of this comes from comparisons of prices in similar countries producing the same products and the many instances of rural raw-material producers smuggling their products into neighboring countries to avoid the low marketing board prices (Bates 1988; Roemer and Jones 1991; Puetz and von Braun 1991).

Borrowing to reduce risk. Borrowing is another crucial risk-sharing strategy, but only if default is permitted upon the failure of the venture. This is because in some lending arrangements repayment must be made, sooner or later. Even if the lender loses some income because of the lateness of the payment, the borrower does not reduce his or her risks through borrowing, but may actually increase the risk because the efforts necessary to repay are so economically damaging. The borrower may simply remain in a permanent state of indebtedness, with obligations to work for the lender, who is often also the large landowner. Many rubber tappers in the Brazilian Amazon are "captured" in this way (Allegretti 1990: 255).

Clearly this no-default arrangement is much more common when individuals borrow from other individuals. There is much evidence that moneylenders (discussed in greater detail later) are often able to reduce their risk of default to close to zero. To take just one example, Kailas Sarap (1991) finds a very low rate of default on loans even to the poorest households in the Indian state of Orissa. This is due not only to the loan terms that require the borrower to work off the debt if it is not paid back on time, and to the borrower's recognition that defaulters have much more difficulty getting loans in the future, but also to the great social embarrassment of being in default. Sarap concludes:

Even in the absence of collaterals, loans are repaid because social forces exert pressure; dishonouring a contract means loss of face for the borrowing household to such an extent that even the poorest household will not do so unless compelled by extreme circumstances. And even such involuntary default is rare. (Sarap 1991: 107).

In contrast, businesses, whether private or communal, can and often do go bankrupt. Thus, if the lesson is that businesses can go bankrupt but families often cannot, then the key is to borrow money through organizations that can take reasonable risks (as judged by themselves and by the lenders) but can default and dissolve if the ventures do not work out, or surrender the control over the forestry venture while shielding the individual households from both economic and social pressure.

Diversification.   Broadening forestry development to cover a wider range of activities not only can produce earlier incomes, it can also reduce economic risk. One of the most important principles of business risk management is to diversify activities so that any single failure will not mean disaster for the enterprise. Diversification of forestry activities has several quite different forms. The three most significant options are primary forest product diversification, downstream diversification, and nonforestry diversification.

Primary forest product diversification means developing and extracting a broader range of forest products. These may be a wider variety of trees. In many countries, only a few tree species are accepted by sawmills or exporters, because facilities for marketing or processing them have not been established. The conditions that encourage or discourage markets for lesser-known tree species depend largely on government policy. In many countries the commercial loggers operating on state-controlled forestland establish the markets for various timber species by the volume of their production. The government's royalty and tax policies have a major impact on how attractive the harvesting and processing of lesser-known species will be for these commercial loggers. For example, if the government's royalties are based on the value of the trees cut rather than on the potential value of the trees on the land, then the loggers will not have incentive to harvest the lesser-known species (Gillis 1988a: 61).

Gathering of nontimber forest products, as long as the user community holds or can obtain appropriate user rights, can also be widely diversified. In the Brazilian Amazon, for example, the rubber tappers who are not beholden to large-scale landowners[3] have been able to diversify their family or multifamily production to include the gathering of Brazil nuts, palm hearts,[4] fruits, and medicinal resins (as well as the agricultural production of manioc, tobacco, and sugarcane). Mary Allegretti concludes that:

> The greater diversification under the autonomous system assures a better quality of life, because these activities are aimed at meeting the actual needs of the family unit. . . . Rubber tapping and gathering of Brazil nuts are carried out during alternate periods of the year and, by selling these products, families can obtain industrial goods that are essential for production or domestic consumption. Additional activities such as agriculture, gathering, hunting, and fishing are all aimed at domestic consumption and are carried out according to the availability of labor within the family unit. (Allegretti 1990: 256)

The downstream diversification strategy is to become involved in more activities for a given forest product. Expansion into the processing and marketing of primary products such as timber, resins, nuts, etc. (often called "downstream processing") has been attractive because of three potentials.

First, greater involvement of the original resource extractor in the processing of the resource may make it possible to capture more of the profits that come from adding value to the raw resource. However, there is certainly no guarantee that expanding the community's processing capacity makes economic sense. Many expansions are justified with the false logic that the mark-up between raw-material prices and intermediate or final prices means profit. This argument ignores the question of costs: how much does the community have to pay, in terms of money and labor, to process raw materials in order to sell them at a higher price? Consider timber processing. The small-scale, often older, sawmill equipment that communities can afford is frequently at a serious disadvantage in its efficiency, compared to the equipment used by larger-scale commercial sawmills. Are community members skilled enough to produce intermediate or final products efficiently and profitably? Harvesters are not necessarily good furniture makers, although they may turn out to be. Would they be as profitable in devoting their money and efforts to this task as devoting themselves to developing and extracting raw forest products? This last question is crucial but often overlooked. The issue is not so much whether a venture is competitive and profitable; it is whether the venture taps into what the community does most productively.

The second potential of downstream diversification is that greater involvement of the original extractor in the marketing of the raw material or its processed products may be able to strengthen the bargaining power of the resource extractor in setting the price to the next buyer of the resource. A single buyer, or even a very limited number of buyers, puts the resource seller at a big disadvantage in bargaining over the sales price. For example, in Honduras there were roughly 100 cooperatives (with a total of around 4,000 members) involved in pine resin extraction in the mid-1908s, but only two buyers in the whole country—a situation that gave the buyers so much bargaining power that the cooperatives' profits were very low (Abt Associates 1990d: 55).[5]

Similarly, Brazilian rubber tappers in remote Amazonian areas may be visited by very few rubber purchasers, who therefore could get away with offering low prices. If this circumstance can be overcome by resource extractors who bypass the middlemen, who otherwise could offer very low bids, then the resource sellers could bargain with the next level in the marketing chain, where perhaps competition in buying the resource could raise the prices. For example, the rubber-purchasing middlemen bring the latex to towns, where there are often numerous processors who have to compete in bidding for the middlemen's supply. If the rubber tappers could organize to purchase boats and hire crews to collect the latex and bring it to the town processors on behalf of the tappers, then the tappers would have the potential to get higher prices.

This second potential has been the allure of many attempts

at processing and marketing cooperatives, often growing out of envy of the middlemen (who sometimes seem to have a relatively easy life) and the widespread belief that middlemen typically capture huge profits. Sometimes it is indeed true that middlemen can dictate the price and can then make a sizable profit in their sale to the next level. When prices go up for more finished products, the prices of primary products are often slow to respond. However, many circumstances lead to different outcomes. First, the apparently great markups imposed by middlemen do not simply represent profit, because the middlemen also face numerous risks. For instance, the boats transporting latex may be lost, the latex may be rejected for low quality, the processors' price may decline before the middleman can get the latex to the town, and so on.

Second, the higher levels of purchasers may also involve few buyers, so that the immediate middleman may also face low prices. For exported products like Brazil nuts or Guatemalan *xate* palm (used in floral arrangements), the least competitive level of buyers may be at the export level itself, restricted to the companies that have the necessary international connections, export licenses, and marketing expertise to find overseas markets. In many instances, it is unrealistic to expect resource extractors to extend their activities right up to the international export stage. Therefore, in deciding whether to extend cooperative efforts to marketing, the cooperative leaders have to make a very sober assessment of the true profits at each stage of the marketing process and of the cooperative's true capabilities. Thus, in addition to the questions of the efficiency of the community's processing is the question of whether the cooperative will be competent at marketing the resource. Marketing takes skills and contacts. It also requires capital to ride out the periods when overall market prices are low or there are unexpected losses.

The third potential is diversification to reduce risk. Downstream diversification can make the community less vulnerable to price downturns of its primary outputs. To the degree that the prices of the processed outputs do not fall along with the prices of the raw outputs, the community can reduce the risk of major losses. For example, if timber prices decline by half, but lumber prices only go down by 25 percent, then the forestry cooperative that owns its own sawmill can partially escape the impact of the decline. A cooperative that owns a sawmill with capacity beyond its own timber production can even take advantage of the lower timber prices under these conditions.

However, spreading the production from raw forest products to intermediate or finished forest products is not necessarily an effective way to diversify. Production would remain within the same sector, which to a certain degree rises or falls as a whole. If the demand for finished products goes down (if, for example, large-scale domestic production expands, or more imports are permitted), the community could well lose out in selling both the raw material and the related finished product. Many people assume that when the prices for the raw material go down, the next stages of processing become more profitable. But the advantage evaporates if the decline in raw material prices is due to declines in the demand and prices of the finished product, which obviously translate into lower revenues. Thus, if the community's objective for diversifying is to reduce its vulnerability, it should consider undertaking less related activities, assuming that these activities are efficient.

The diversification beyond extracting forest products strategy is to combine forestry with activities that do not involve the extraction of forest products. These activities span a wide range, from developing nature-oriented tourism ("eco-tourism") and game reserves to raising livestock. In terms of reducing risks, this form of diversification has the advantage over forest-product diversification and downstream diversification that the people involved are less exposed if the whole forestry sector suffers a major setback or forest user rights are disrupted. The most prominent broadening is agroforestry—the combination of agricultural and forestry activities, covering both the introduction of crops within forestland and the planting of trees on farms.

The initial challenge to agroforestry was that either alternative—all agriculture or all managed forest (largely plantations)—seemed to be more efficient and productive. Uniform planting is easier to do; so are maintenance and harvesting of single, uniform crops. If land is good enough for annual crops, why reduce their volume to make way for trees? If land is not good enough for annual crops, but suits trees, why not pick the most profitable species and concentrate on that?

The counterarguments come from both biology and economics. On productive farmland, trees can actually enhance certain annual food crops and perennial cash crops by providing shade, protection from wind and soil erosion, and "living fences." Trees and shrubs can suppress weeds and help to recycle nutrients into the soil (Nair 1992). Plantations of single species are sometimes less productive because of diseases and pest damage that would be less if the trees were more mixed and same-species trees were separated by greater distances (Kanowski and Savill 1992). Under some conditions, crops planted among trees provide their own produce without reducing the growth of the trees.

From an economic perspective, agroforestry insulates producers from a drop in the price of any particular crop as well as physical threats to each crop. It also allows for a more efficient use of labor, because people can keep occupied during more periods of the year, and the reduction of volume for any one crop makes a labor shortage for planting or harvesting that crop less likely. Appropriate degrees of agriculture and grazing on state-owned forestland can also provide food and incomes for landless or land-poor farmers.

Agroforestry ought to be considered like other technologies: it has strong promise, but also it has risks. There has been considerable progress in learning about what mixtures of trees and faster-growing crops can be combined, where different agroforestry approaches may work, and what management practices make sense.[6] Agroforestry requires knowledge and organization, which, again, can be provided by user-group organizations, government, nongovernmental organizations, or all three.

Reducing uncertainty.

The root of uncertainty is lack of information. It is not just that some forestry developments fail because of ignorance of market conditions, soil conditions, technologies, government policies, etc.; many forest users shrink from truly promising developments because lack of information increases the level of risk that they feel. In Honduras, for example, the practice of pine resin tapping—an extractive activity that is sustainable because modern resin-tapping methods can keep a tree productive for up to forty years—has been abandoned in certain areas because the tappers do not know whether the wide swings in prices will allow them to sell their resin profitably. In addition, the cartel that buys much of the resin rejects some low-quality resin, so tappers working in marginal woodlands often do not know ahead of time whether the resin they extract will be purchased. In abandoning these trees for resin tapping, several cooperatives have begun to cut them for firewood (Stanley 1991: 31).

By pooling their resources, community groups can make enormous progress in improving their information and technical expertise. The Kuna Indians of Panama, for example, have succeeded brilliantly in establishing a forest park reserve that makes money from tourism, scientific research, and donations from international nongovernmental organizations and governments. To handle all of the complexities of dealing with the Panamanian government, international tourists, scientific organizations, suppliers, etc., the Kuna pay for the advice of international advisers (Clay 1988: 66–67).

Even the most skeptical critics of the spread of government acknowledge the importance of government's function in providing better information, since good information is a necessary condition for efficient markets. Therefore governments must overcome the natural worry that free access to information may bring to light embarrassing issues—such as the failures of some government programs.

Small-scale experiments as a form of learning and information. Separate plots devoted to different species, different mixes of species, and different forestry practices provide not only separation and variety to reduce risk, but also *learning.* So do small-scale, exploratory ventures in marketing or processing. These trial runs, or prototypes, reduce uncertainty by establishing a performance record for each option, without the huge costs and risks of a full-scale operation. Both of these alternatives require organization to plan and to exercise discipline, because one option will often appear to be more attractive, leading some people to question experimenting with other alternatives. Therefore the hedging strategies of launching several modest experiments require a firm, long-term perspective on how to handle risk.

Earlier income opportunities.

The major types of strategies for providing earlier income opportunities from forestry activities include faster-growing trees, extracting wood from the trees before they are mature, and providing incomes for forestry development in addition to forestry exploitation.

Faster-growing trees. A seemingly straightforward way to bring forward the payoff period of forest development is to rely on faster-growing species. Research has identified a host of fast-growing species, such as eucalyptus and gmelina, originating from different world regions. Technology has developed even faster-growing varieties within already fast-growing species.

Yet there are important physical risks involved with introducing and relying on fast-growing species. First, if the trees are planted close to one another, as in plantations, there is a higher chance of infestation by pests that specialize in that tree species. Many naturally occurring trees are dispersed widely in the forest, avoiding the spread of these specialized pests.

Second, if the fast-growing species are not native to the area (exotics), they may face great risk of disease or poor growth. In some cases, exotic tree species are less susceptible to the pests in a particular area, because pests that become specialized in preying on that species are lacking (Zobel, van Wyk, and Stahl 1987; Kanowski and Savill 1992). However, planting exotic species sometimes backfires, often only after massive investments. Their growth may be disappointing because essential nutrients turn out to be lacking in the soils.[7] Sometimes local pests suddenly explode to wipe out an entire planting of exotics.

Third, exotic species sometimes have unanticipated

impacts on the whole ecosystem. Eucalyptus, for example, have drawn down the water tables at surprising rates in some places. Some fast-growing species, again including eucalyptus, contain chemicals that are noxious to birds, insects, and animals. Stands of these trees are very poor habitats for wildlife. The fact that exotics can be invasive, moving into areas not intended for them, adds another dimension to the environmental risks. Research has been addressing these problems by identifying the conditions for relatively safe introduction of exotic species, while at the same time identifying fast-growing *native* species and the best conditions for planting and protecting these species.[8]

Harvesting wood before maturity.   Other techniques for hastening the returns on timber itself include selective pruning of branches for firewood and harvesting for poles rather than for sawn timber. As sensible as these techniques may be if done with restraint, there is the danger that their availability will provoke their unrestrained use. This can lead to forest degradation even if large trees are not cut, since overharvesting of young trees and branches can stifle the regeneration needed to replace old trees.

Extraction of nontimber forest products.   Forest products other than timber are often immediately or soon available for harvesting, whether the forest users are actually planting these resources or simply gathering them from within forest reserves or newly forested areas. Fruits, resins, nuts, flowers, and bark are often available long before trees reach harvestable size; nontree species that grow or live within the forest, even if it is newly established, are also available earlier than the timber. These range from palm fronds to game meat.

Some recent studies have gone so far as to claim that the economic value of nontimber forest products can far outweigh the timber value of the forest and the proceeds from converting forestland into other uses, thus making a strong argument for maintaining natural forests. Efforts to show the surprisingly great value of nontimber resources have been applied to regions as diverse as the Amazon, Central America, and

Indonesia (Anderson and Jardim 1989; Alcorn 1989; Peters, Gentry, and Mendelsohn 1989; Gomez-Pompa and Kaus 1990; Gillis 1988a). Other studies have cautioned against too much optimism, since theoretical calculations of what a hectare of land could yield may diverge greatly from the actual yield permitted by markets and management practices (Browder 1990; Salafsky, Dugelby, and Terborgh 1993).

Yet even if nontimber extraction is not a big moneymaker, it is an obvious source of income supplement while the forests exist and has clear effects on winning over the extractors to the idea that they should conserve the forest. It is therefore remarkable that many governments have neglected or even discouraged nontimber extraction. For example, in pre-independence Kenya, the British colonial government frequently denied permits to local Kikuyu people living in the southern Mount Kenya region to gather medicinal plants, deadwood, and honey from the crown forests that had recently been their own communal land (Castro 1988: 41).[9] Many observers have remarked on the disinterest of governments to promote nontimber development and extraction in Mexico, India, Malaysia, and other countries.[10]

Drawing earlier income through development activities. A well-organized forestry community can buffer the incomes of its most economically vulnerable members by assigning them the development tasks that command continuous payment. These include the tasks of operating the nurseries, weeding, guarding, constructing and maintaining trails, etc. The organizational requirements for assigning these income-earning tasks to the most vulnerable are assessed in Chapter 4.

Liquidating forest investment without liquidating the forest. If forest users anticipate that they might need income before forest resources reach maturity, it is important for them to have the ongoing choice of keeping their investments in long-term forestry development or cashing out their investments earlier. This would have to be an ongoing option, rather than a once-and-for-all decision at the time the project is launched, because the forest users do not know ahead of time whether they will need income earlier than the maturity of the project. As mentioned in Chapter 2, the two major options are borrowing and selling.

Credit and borrowing. Borrowing off of the future value of the forestry assets can be conducted within or outside of the community. Community organizations can establish emergency loan funds to help members during difficult periods, especially if the emergency cash problems come from circumstances, such as illnesses or weddings, that generally do not affect the bulk of community families at the same time. The risk of deliberate default on such loans is generally very low, because of the social pressures that other community members can apply to the borrower and because the borrower's opportunity to take part in further forestry (or other) activities within the community's operations is a form of collateral. Community loan funds can also provide small-scale financing for members' private economic ventures: to buy a wagon, saplings, fencing materials, etc. If community members know that such funds will be available if and when a promising investment opportunity arises, they will be more content to keep their own savings tied up in forest development.

Lending within close-knit communities sometimes has the problem that communities of kin, friends, and neighbors often feel pressures to lend to one another at very low or zero interest rates. Sometimes this is a justifiable and compassionate practice. However, it creates a challenge to discourage borrowing for unnecessary personal spending and unwise investments. Borrowing at very low interest rates eats away at the savings of those who feel compelled to lend and permits investments in ventures of questionable economic value. (World Bank 1990: 113). Therefore another reason for creating more formal loan funds within community organizations is that enterprising, savings-conscious members of the community can refer personal requests for loans to the community loan fund, where proper screening and reasonable interest rates can be applied.

Nevertheless, community forestry operations are not often

blessed with big treasuries, especially during the start-up period before their forest resources are yielding high revenues. Therefore community members often have to look outside of their kin and their fellow community members to find credit. How can they be confident, before they engage in forestry investments, that this credit will be available at reasonable interest rates?

The three outside options are typically the area's private moneylenders, the private banks, and the government. Because of the key role of competition, the presence of more than one is generally very important.

Private informal credit. Private moneylenders are very controversial. There has been a widespread view that moneylenders in developing countries charge outrageously high interest rates that worsen the economic situation of the borrower, sometimes to the point that borrowers end up losing whatever property or user rights they held before they sought credit, whether for investment or to cover emergencies. Moneylenders therefore often face the same criticism as the merchant middlemen discussed previously. Indeed, the situation for moneylenders is often worse, because governments frequently ban their operation.[11] Some studies of the actual profits of moneylenders and their importance in providing credit have led to a very different, much more positive assessment:

> Not long ago moneylenders were regarded as parasites who exploited impoverished peasants. Today one reads instead of how informal lenders provide efficient financial services to a broad clientele that is badly served by formal sector intermediaries. . . . Fueling this transformation of opinion is a growing body of research demonstrating that [informal financial intermediaries] are less exploitative than formerly assumed, and indeed quite well suited to administering financial services in small doses. Research has established, too, that formal sector loan programs for "priority" groups such as small and medium enterprises . . . are often costly failures, even to

the point of undermining the financial health of the [financial intermediaries] involved." (Bolnick 1992: 57)

The reality seems to be much more varying and complicated. In some situations, the interest rates charged by moneylenders reflect their costs and risks; in other cases the interest rates are very high even taking into account their costs and risks. [12] Even where government and private-bank credit is available, many people prefer to borrow from informal, unregulated sources despite the usually higher interest rates. This is because these sources can lend more quickly, they can make small loans, and they often allow much more flexibility in the use of the borrowed money (Bolnick 1992: 63).

The key factor that seems to explain whether private credit sources charge reasonable or excessive interest rates is competition. Studies show that where borrowers have access to more than one lending source, the interest rates come to reflect actual costs and risks (Aleem 1990; Iqbal 1988). One careful assessment of lending throughout rural India found that the presence of a bank in a village significantly reduces the interest rates charged by moneylenders (Iqbal 1988: 374). These results suggest that community organizations' loan funds can serve a useful purpose even beyond the limited amounts that can be gathered from community members, because they can provide a form of competition with the private moneylenders. Government lending programs can serve the same purpose, if they are managed carefully as outlined later.

Private banks can lend to both community organizations for forestry activities and to households within the community. The well-known drawbacks of formal banks are their tendencies to make big rather than small loans (because a few big loans can involve as much money as many small ones, with less effort needed to examine and approve the large loans); to make long-term rather than short-term loans (for the same reason of less costs to examine and approve the loans); to prefer borrowers with solid collateral; to take moderately long periods to decide on loans (as compared to informal moneylenders); and to lend within the bankers' social and political groups, which rarely include low-income forest users.

The clear lesson is that community organizations can generally qualify better for private bank loans than can individual members of the community. Both the size of the loan and the combined collateral of the community organization will make its loan application more attractive. By borrowing some of the investment funds needed for forest development, the community organization can reduce the risks faced by community members. In addition, the examination by the bankers may yield useful advice concerning the wisdom of the organization's plans—it can be an inexpensive source of technical assistance.

Government lending, if motivated by the goal of providing credit to small-scale activities of lower-income people, can go where private lenders are not interested. Rural credit is a feature of most governments' policies. As mentioned, government credit can provide competition for private moneylenders. Government banks, like private banks, can also be instrumental in financing the forestry operations of user collectives.

To try to make its credit efforts more impressive, and to gain more political support, governments often provide rural credit at interest rates below the rates that the free market for loans would call for. Yet cheap credit from the government carries an alarming number of problems.[13] Low interest rates mean that the government cannot afford to provide cheap credit for everyone, so the loans end up being rationed. People with the best connections to the officials responsible for lending therefore have a strong advantage. In many cases, only people with official land titles can qualify for government loans. In countries where titles require demonstration that land has been "improved," such as Costa Rica, this has actually led to the destruction of natural forests in order to qualify for government loans! To keep costs low in the face of the money-losing proposition of lending at low rates, official banks often prefer to make big loans rather than small, since a few big loans take less staff time than many small ones. These factors make it difficult for the poor to get the loans.

Cheap credit has also been linked to land-use distortions and poor forestry practices. Cheap credit available to rural people is often an inducement to try to convert forests into agriculture; partly to have a project to qualify for the loans, partly because cheap credit makes otherwise unattractive investments seem artificially attractive.

In Costa Rica the credit subsidies for livestock increased steadily into the 1980s; several laws for rescheduling debts of farmers and ranchers increased the effective subsidies even more in the late 1980s. These policies mainly favored large cattle ranchers, leading to both the conversion of good agricultural land into less worthwhile pasture and the clearing of land that should have been left forested (Lutz and Daly 1990: 13–16).

On the other hand, if cheap credit is reserved or earmarked for forestry activities, it may have the harmful effect of drawing inappropriate people into forest exploitation. Many people with no experience in sustainable forestry would be tempted to take advantage of cheap credit.

There is even a risk that cheap government credit could *raise* the interest rates for poor people. If the government provides cheap loans, but cannot fulfill all of the demand for these loans, then the moneylenders will have a narrower group of clients. If, as is often the case, the borrowers who do not qualify for government loans are the most economically vulnerable people, then the risk facing the moneylenders (that is, that borrowers may default) may actually go up, requiring higher interest rates to offset this risk (Iqbal 1988: 371).

Another drawback of cheap official credit is that the apparently lower interest rates of official credit from government agencies may actually mask the need of the borrower to provide kickbacks or bribes to the bank officials in order to qualify for the loans (Iqbal 1988: 377; World Bank 1990: Chapter 7). In other words, the subsidies in interest rates may be subsidizing the borrowers less than appears, or not at all; instead they may be subsidizing the officials involved in making the loan decisions.

Early sale of the land or user rights is the most direct way for forest users to cash in on future earnings when immediate cash is needed. Both private forest users and communities have sold trees and land on innumerable occasions, both where it is legally permitted and where it is not. After all, quiet agreements among people as to who can work a particular piece of land can be made regardless of legal bans. However, there are many cases in which the forest user may wish to sell forest products before they are ready to be extracted and yet does not want to sell the user rights (or the land). Similarly, the buyer may be content to have the product and not wish to pay for user rights beyond a particular sale. Therefore a wide variety of mechanisms for selling partial future harvesting rights or a share of future proceeds has been developed. [14]

The peculiar risk associated with arrangements for sales of future shares or harvesting rights is that the value of the deal for the buyer depends on the assurance that the arrangement will be honored. This is one reason why legal recognition of the right to sell is important: even if a nonlegal sale can be arranged, neither the buyer nor the seller can have the same degree of confidence that the deal will be honored. To the degree that community or government actions can establish a stable rule of law, buyers can be confident that future proceeds are worth buying. When this legal recognition and stability are present, remarkably long-term agreements can be made— which can thereby bring the benefits to the forest developers very close to the beginning of their efforts. Perhaps the most striking case is from feudal Japan, where there was sufficient stability and recognition of contracts from 1600 to the mid-1800s to allow rural villages to enter into formal agreements on proceed-sharing of timber sales as much as fifty years into the future (McKean 1993: 72).

Reducing the general economic insecurity of forest users.

Beyond the risks of specific forestry ventures, it is often the overall insecurity of the forest user that drives the irresponsible exploitation of forests. As mentioned previously, the preference for immediate income, and the short time horizons that this preference demands, make every long-term investment less attractive and any risk loom larger. For sustainable forestry management, the fundamental problem of poverty alleviation is not just a matter of the average income levels of poor people, but also a question of income security.

Income security can be addressed by the principles of sharing within a community, as they establish the community's obligations to aid its members in greatest need. In addition, any community or government strategy that securely improves the incomes of the very poor, or simply smoothes out or steadies their income flows, can contribute to greater incentives to focus on long-term sustainability.

Policy Reforms: What Governments Should (and Should Not) Do

The problems and strategies reviewed in this chapter reveal that governments and government policies can be the source of the economic risks to sustainable small-scale forestry activities—or part of the solution. Governments, especially if they are overly ambitious and overly controlling, can create the conditions that greatly worsen the obstacles and risks that small-scale forest users face. These include low prices for forest products, greater price uncertainty, insecure user rights, loss of user rights, exclusion by commercial loggers, scarcity of credit, shorter time horizons among the forest users, and cumbersome regulations that require great effort or even force people into illegal activities.

Government should stay out of the businesses of:

- marketing forest products

- rationing cheap credit.

Government should also avoid the heavy-handed regulations of:

- prohibiting middlemen and moneylenders

- forcing downstream diversification by restricting markets

- restricting rights to sell or use assets as collateral

- prohibiting nontimber forest products extraction, even from state-controlled land

- imposing policies that make certain land uses artificially attractive.

Government should be very wary about:

- leasing state-controlled land to commercial loggers, who might exclude traditional users

- excluding small-scale forest users from state-controlled land even for the sake of conservation.

However, there are many functions of government that are useful without requiring heavy intervention. These are:

- upholding appropriate boundaries

- enforcing rules against spillover damage when the communities cannot resolve these conflicts

- helping the development of private credit institutions

- providing credit at market rates

- supporting research and technological development

- providing technical assistance and training

- providing market information

- aiding diversification by easing the bureaucratic obstacles to entering into new activities and markets

- entering into joint ventures with communities lacking sufficient internal resources or capacity to borrow

- undertaking general poverty alleviation programs.

Beyond specific functions, it is important for governments to provide a rather stable environment with clear signals of its policy intentions. This is necessary to reduce "government risk": the possibility that the government will change the conditions that affect profitability.

Clearly the supportive actions and policies of government require more restraint and discipline than the actions and policies we are advising against. Who will fill the vacuum? For almost every risk-reducing strategy, the numerical strength and organizing potential of community groups hold clear promise. This is the premise that leads us to the next chapter's focus on community organization.

4 Approaches to Community Organization

This chapter explores the design requirements for effective community action to create and manage forest resources. Community organization is often the best approach for overcoming the individual selfishness, governmental dominance, and lack of enforcement that mar so many failed forest management efforts. Community organization is often the only counterweight to efforts to take the user rights away from individuals and families whose meager incomes depend on forest exploitation. Community organization is also often the most effective institution for defining and maintaining individual and family rights of members of the community. Five different community forestry challenges are outlined, along with the problems that typically arise for each and the approaches that may help to deal with these problems.

Before examining these five challenges, it is useful to explore the meaning of the central ideas of "community," "organization," and "user group." "Community" has at least two common meanings. It can mean the people who live within a geographical area. This definition leaves open the question of whether the people within a geographical area actually share in a spirit of community in the sense of *common* interests and *common* identification. Therefore we find it is more useful to define community in terms of the people who have a sense of common interest and identification, growing out of shared characteristics. One of these characteristics, which usually overlaps with others, is the traditional use of specific forest resources. We believe that it is more reasonable to expect that people with common interests, generally linked to their work, will behave as unified communities. In contrast, there are many studies that show that populations living in the same geographical area often consist of subgroups with quite opposing interests and no basis for common or joint action. Governments and local elites might hope that everyone within a geographical area will behave as a community, but that rarely happens.

We presume further that shared rights to use particular forest resources provide the potential for a sense of common interest and identification. When a set of individuals or families has a history or tradition of exercising these rights, their sense of community is even more likely. Indeed, the set of users—a "user group"—is often connected by common ethnic, religious, or caste background. Sometimes the user group is literally defined by clan or family ties. The original inhabitants of sparsely populated forest areas often belong to small, ethnically and culturally separate groups that are very distinct from the larger populations of the country, who often entered the area in rather recent waves of migration. To these newcomers, the original forest users are the "tribals," the "indigenous people," or the "aboriginals," to be regarded with a mixture of sympathy, paternalism, and contempt.

In other cases, the customary forest users are simply families or clans that have established claims to various forest uses. Ironically, in these cases it is sometimes harder for the outside world, including government and nongovernmental organizations, to realize that not everyone within a geographical area is the same in terms of traditional rights to access to the forest. Of course, we do not assume that people with shared interests in using particular forest resources will necessarily act together; that is the purpose of organizing.

User groups are best defined according to specific forest resources in a given area. The same forest area may have many different groups of people, each with a history of extracting or otherwise using particular resources, for their own use or to sell to others. One group may have been cutting one species of tree; another tapping rubber or resin; another burning forest plots to plant crops; yet another foraging its livestock in the same forest area. To the degree that other people in the area and the government recognize that this historical use gives the user group the right to continue to extract or use the resource, the group is said to have a "customary right."

This seemingly simple situation has three very serious complications. First, individuals or groups, with or without government backing, often assert ownership claims for a particular piece of land and the resources on it. "Ownership" is often taken to mean that the owner can dispose of the land and all of its resources in any way he or she sees fit, with the possible exception that the government may restrict some uses or require others for the public good. Obviously, ownership claims can conflict with specific user-right claims in the same area. In addition, ownership can be very misleading if it seems to imply that one unit, whether it is an individual, family, group, or government, necessarily holds all of the rights to use any or all of the resources in a given area. It is much more useful to think in terms of specific rights.

Second, an obvious source of conflict facing a given traditional user group is that neither the government nor other people in the area will necessarily accept previous use as an acceptable claim for the right to continued use. In fact, as the next chapter argues, one of the biggest problems is that many governments have viewed traditional forest uses as either harmful or inconvenient and therefore have rejected the claims of user groups to their customary rights. The exclusive ownership claims of newcomers, including commercial logging companies, are often viewed sympathetically by the government because these newcomers are more ethnically and culturally similar to the government officials than the formerly isolated natives. The original inhabitants often lack (at least at first) the sophistication, language skills, and contacts with the world outside of their area to be effective in fighting for their rights or getting the greatest economic benefits from their exploitation of the forest.

Third, various circumstances sometimes throw together users who have little in common. Governments, for example, may allow or even encourage people beyond the traditional users to try to exploit the same resources. Similarly, migration may bring in people who use the resources despite their lack of traditional or customary rights, with or without government approval, or new forms of forest exploitation may attract people who do not share common experience or roots. This means that the whole set of users may not constitute a true community in the sense of common interests, common identifications, and community spirit. Thus, the set of users is not necessarily a true "group," in the sense of having some degree of unity of action. Yet the resource users, particularly if they have shared a long period of exploiting the same resource, have the greatest promise to develop into a true community of common interests, identity, and action. This, in turn, requires organization.

A "community organization" is any arrangement for collective action by a particular set of individuals or families. Community organizations can be designed to serve everyone within a particular geographical area, or specific types of individuals and families. Again, we argue that the most effective community organizations will be based on common interests arising from common work, not on the mere fact of living in the same area. Therefore this chapter will focus largely on organizations of communities of forest users, meaning the people who use the same forest resources. The rubber tappers and ranchers now locked in a bloody struggle in the Brazilian Amazon are all forest users, but they cannot be considered as part of the same community of users in any meaningful sense.

The Importance of Collective Nongovernmental Action

Why should we be concerned with promoting community action, or, for that matter, group action of any kind? Why not just let each individual or family operate in its own separate interests? It should be clear from previous chapters that one of the main reasons why people overexploit the forest is that they have no reason to believe that others would not do the same. Each individual is left with the worry that his or her self-discipline would be a foolish self-sacrifice, since others would feel free to deplete the forest resource. But if some higher authority could coordinate and discipline all (or at least most) individuals with access rights, then individual self-discipline makes sense.

There are two obvious ways to provide the higher authority. Often, government has tried to serve this role. Yet government authority over natural resources has its own problems. These include corruption, rigid rules, and indifference to local knowledge, needs, and desires. When the government imposes restrictions on forest exploitation, it often creates conflicts with community members because of the gulf between local communities and the authorities, who are often based in faraway national or provincial capitals. In many countries, the government is too weak, or devotes too few resources, to police the forests effectively. The typical result is that the forests are controlled in name by the central or provincial government, but in fact they are hardly controlled or regulated at all. The same dangerous situation of open access holds, even though on paper forest uses are severely restricted. In many cases the government can enforce restrictions only by having guards physically present throughout the forest and then prosecuting the violators, yet this is far too costly for most governments to do. In the late 1970s, for example, before community forestry was introduced, there was a backlog of 50,000 cases of forest offenses pending before the government in the Pakistani-controlled Azad Kashmir area.

The second possibility is the authority of the forest user community itself, acting collectively. Community organization has strong potential to overcome the logic that drives individuals to overuse forest resources. A community can often enforce responsible forest uses without devoting tremendous financial and manpower resources, since it can often depend on social pressure and community spirit rather than armed guards. Community organizations can often find strength in numbers in their relations with the government, especially when the government pays too little attention to what the community wants and needs.

Risks and Costs of Community Action

These considerations certainly support the logic of community forestry, but they do not magically solve the community's problem of how to organize effectively and sustainably. Efforts in community management of forest resources can have serious costs, and their success is by no means guaranteed. Because of the promise of community action, many communities have leaped into collective action, sometimes without realizing the problems that can emerge. Community action can be a complicated, frustrating, and sometimes dangerous undertaking. Community groups often require hard work with little personal reward for the activists. Even the best intentions sometimes cannot prevent community groups from falling apart. There are even occasions when the worst enemies of the community are lurking within it. Sometimes wealthy and powerful local people continue to dominate, leaders of community forestry cooperatives steal the organization's money, or a few individuals end up owning much of the land that was to be awarded to the community as a whole.

Activism also often means conflict with outsiders who are excluded from group benefits. For reasons explained in greater detail later, community action must establish boundaries between those entitled to benefit from community action and those who are not; otherwise the openness of access to benefits will discourage people in the core group from devoting adequate effort. It is understandable, therefore, that the outsiders often resent being excluded.

It is also rather common for community leaders (and government officials) to operate as if community participation means only cooperation, mutual interest, and permanent goodwill. Naturally, the appeal to cooperation is an important ingredient in the campaign to launch community-based projects. Yet the fact is that conflicts do arise. When they do, community-action arrangements that do not provide for clear ways to resolve conflicts are open to bitter confrontation.

Activism may also arouse the hostility of the government, if government officials come to believe that the community group threatens their power and ability to govern. One rationale for organizing community groups is to overcome the typical government tendencies either to keep the forests completely off-limits or to look to commercial loggers to exploit the forests. By the same token, the community groups are likely to be seen as threats to the government's plans and therefore may be ignored or even suppressed. In addition, many government policies are based on the assumption that the government is dealing with individuals, companies, or entire legal units (such as villages, counties, districts, etc.). Property is typically assigned to individuals or to government subunits; individuals (or companies treated by the legal system as individuals) are the focus of most regulation and qualify for most benefits offered by governments. Therefore community organizations must also cope with the need to gain some form of recognition and cooperation from governments that are often unused to dealing with collective groups rather than single individuals or firms.

In short, community action to secure forest rights, and to use the forests as a collective effort, is not an easy task that can be launched without careful thought and preparation. By assessing the major difficulties, we can try to outline how a careful approach can avoid these pitfalls.

The logic (as well as simple good feelings) of launching a community activity often tempts leaders representing geographical or legal units, as well as government officials, to define "community" very broadly. If these leaders are trying to gain consensus and cooperation, they typically wish to avoid antagonizing anyone and therefore to avoid making it clear that some individuals or groups are *not* to be included. Yet the original forest users obviously often try to restrict the relevant community to themselves—those with a history of particular kinds of forest exploitation. This may make good sense, if broader participation means diluting the benefits to the point that people with user rights have too little incentive to care for the resource base responsibly. Yet outsiders, leaders representing geographical or legal units, and government officials may well regard this attitude as selfish and destructive of their plans to engage in broader community cooperation. This difference in defining the boundaries of community can lead to many problems: open access if the broadening goes too far; loss of support from the outside authorities if they see the community as too narrow; and conflict between the narrower community and the broader community regardless of the outcome.

Types of Community Forestry Undertakings

Communities face different opportunities of afforestation, reforestation, and forest use. Some community forestry efforts are entirely within the control of a given community (defined according to one of the definitions discussed previously), and others inevitably involve other groups and institutions. If a town or village decides to create a woodlot on communal land, for example, the community itself may be the sole actor. In such cases, whether or not the community can work together to operate the woodlot in a constructive and sustainable way has to do with its internal relationships and the competence of its leadership. In other cases, community forestry efforts are much more complicated because of the involvement of other people and institutions—neighboring communities, the government, and commercial enterprises including logging companies. Therefore there are important differences between community action of a political nature—efforts to gain governmental recognition of community organizations and to obtain the rights to control forests—and the design of the community forestry organizations themselves. In light of these differences, the logic of community action obviously has to differ according to the nature of the undertaking.

Five types of undertakings are important:

1. *Obtaining user rights for existing resource use opportunities*—gaining recognition from the government (and possibly other groups) for the community's right to use the resource, including the rights to harvest timber, extract nontimber products such as nuts or resin, gather fuelwood, and graze livestock. This often involves gaining access to secondary products of forests for which the government reserves timber harvesting either for itself or for commercial loggers.

2. *Defending existing user rights and restrictions*—maintaining the right to continue to use the resource, including:

- blocking any government efforts to take over the management of the resource

- restricting outsiders from using the resource, which could deteriorate into an open-access situation that encourages overexploitation

- limiting community members from overusing the resource

3. *Obtaining user rights for state-created resource use opportunities*—qualifying for involvement (and possibly management roles) in government programs and projects to:

- establish sawmills and other downstream processing

- create buffer zones around protected reserves, which offer employment opportunities for community members

- reforest degraded areas with financial incentives provided by the government

4. *Expanding the resource base*—internal efforts to improve the forest resource base, such as:

- conducting community-led reforestation efforts

- establishing and managing community woodlots

- launching park- and tourism-related facilities and services

5. *Expanding the processing capacity for existing resource uses*—establishing downstream activities to process, transport, and market forest products already harvested or gathered by the community, including sawmills, resin refineries, transportation systems, and marketing cooperatives.

Contrasting these five quite different types of activities reveals the wide differences in the degree to which community forestry activities are political. The first two categories are clearly and directly political; politics is the struggle over who gets what (Lasswell 1936). Whenever a community has to organize itself to guard its rights against claims by others, whether they are other private groups or the government, the situation is inevitably political. The same holds within the community whenever the community needs to restrict some members from overexploiting the resource. The third category, obtaining user rights created by government initiatives, is political at least in the respects that other groups are likely to be competing for these opportunities and appeals to the government are essential. Such competition naturally takes on a political face in many cases.

The primary considerations relating to the fourth and fifth categories are more economic than political. That is because the efforts to expand the resource base and related income-generating opportunities go beyond the preexisting, valuable resource-use opportunities—the question is whether such expansions will truly be economically sensible. However, organizing the community so that these efforts can be successful (if the economic logic indeed holds), and learning how to share the fruits of economic success, also have political aspects.

The differences in the logic of dealing with situations across these five categories are so important that the rest of the chapter is organized to deal with each category separately.

Community Challenges and Strategies

Obtaining user rights for existing resource use opportunities.

No matter how noble it sounds to say that all people should share in natural resources, the harsh reality is that many resources would be severely overexploited if access were granted to everyone. Both for resources to be conserved, and for there to be sufficient motivation for people to participate actively in community groups, there must be clear boundaries of membership and area. Whether user rights are linked to land tenure or to more restricted notions of specific resource extraction rights, they have to be held with some degree of exclusivity by a user community. Often, these rights have to be recognized or sanctioned by the government.

Therefore the problem of interacting with the government is central to the challenge of qualifying for resource use rights when the community has not yet firmed up its claims. Regardless of whether the state can make any credible claim as a competent forest manager, the fact is that in most countries the government has already laid claim to most or even all forestlands. Even when a community has had a long tradition of using the forest, community groups typically have to get the government to grant them user rights. In many cases, the community user rights are embedded within government ownership, control, or activity. For example, government plantations may restrict timber harvesting to the government or to commercial loggers, but still grant community rights to gather nuts, branches, leaf litter, or palm fronds among the commercial timber trees. In such cases the government almost always presumes that since the primary forest uses are in government hands, it is the government's authority to assign the rights to secondary forest uses. Government officials often make this assumption despite the fact that the community may have a long history of using the forest this way.

When community groups try to secure these rights, they often confront government agencies that prefer to grant logging concessions to large-scale commercial logging enterprises, usually from outside of the local community. In many instances the concessions give commercial loggers *exclusive* rights to the concession areas, turning the community members into illegal encroachers if they try to exploit the forests in these areas.

The attraction of this strategy for the government is rather obvious. The commercial loggers are usually prepared to pay large royalties to the government, while community forestry is often smaller scale and cannot produce the large surpluses that could be shared with the government. Governments typically believe that the commercial logging companies are competent, or at least more competent than small-scale operations, to exploit the trees efficiently. This is often not true, since the heavy equipment and hasty harvesting of commercial loggers frequently cause enormous damage to other trees that are ruined for later harvesting, but the belief persists in many cases anyway. Logging by large-scale concessionaires often reflects a veiled policy by the government to liquidate the forests for the immediate cash value of the trees—which is then shared by the logging companies and the government.

Just as importantly, commercial logging companies are also often prepared to undertake special projects that the government officials want to be accomplished but would find it difficult or embarrassing to do themselves. In 1990–1991, for example, two multimillion-dollar Indonesian forestry groups reportedly covered US$420 million in foreign-exchange losses of the Bank Duta, which is largely owned by foundations connected with President Suharto. Logging interests are also believed to have paid for the Taman Mini theme park monorail at the behest of the president's wife, financed Suharto's biography, and accepted the president's son and daughter into joint partnerships (Schwarz and Friedland 1992: 42).

There is some cause for optimism, though. The latest trend in many countries is disappointment with private loggers and the cancellation of logging concessions to these private companies. This trend obviously opens up opportunities for local community groups to petition for forest-use rights. In Mexico, for example, the state of Oaxaca canceled private loggers' concessions in 1981, leading to intense and sometimes successful efforts by community groups to gain user rights. In Honduras, the government is giving serious thought to privatizing all trees on private land, reversing the 1974 nationalization of trees.

Finding allies.   Fortunately, community groups have some resources and potential allies in their efforts to gain access to the forests. Their capacity to draw attention to the plight of poor rural people denied their traditional rights can be very important if done with enough restraint to avoid pushing the government into strong antagonism toward the community's movement. There is also a growing disillusionment within many governments over governmental control of forests, as the evidence mounts that state-owned forests have been subject to rapid deforestation, heavy corruption, and international embarrassment.

The allies include various agencies within the governments themselves. No government speaks with a single voice, and within every government there are agencies and individuals in conflict over policies and power. For every powerful forestry agency that is trying to reserve forest exploitation for its favorite commercial logging companies, there are other government agencies, often including a powerful finance ministry, that are trying to break the connection so that the forestry agency (and often the politicians allied with it) cannot control the government's share of the profits arising from forest exploitation.

There are also agencies with the specific mandate or responsibility to assist the community groups. In many instances they are not terribly powerful agencies by themselves, and indeed they may have been created to deflect criticism of the government by giving the appearance that it is addressing the problems of the rural poor. The Brazilian government's Institute for the Defense of the Forest and the National Indian Foundation, for example, are responsible for looking after, among other things, the forestry rights of indigenous communities. During the rapid expansion of Amazonian colonization and forest conversion during the 1970s and 1980s, however, these agencies were given a very small fraction of the budget devoted to Amazonian development; for instance, the mammoth Polonoroeste Project for Rondonia earmarked only 3 percent of the budget for these agencies, compared to 26 percent for the colonization agency (Ascher and Healy 1990: 84–87). However, in cooperation with other government units that are committed to loosening the grip of large commercial logging companies, the influence of such agencies can still be significant.

In some circumstances community movements can also rely on nongovernmental organizations that draw in activists from outside of the community. These NGOs not only can increase the visibility of the community's demands, they can also lend legal and political expertise, as well as increasing the credibility that the community groups will be able to exploit the forests in a reasonable fashion.

International organizations and the donor agencies of industrial countries are also very important potential allies. They, too, can provide the technical expertise in the pursuit of forest-use rights and in the exploitation of the forests, or finance the government's programs to provide technical expertise to community forestry organizations.

Most importantly, international donors can change the economic logic of the government forestry agencies. When an international agency such as the World Bank or the U.S. Agency for International Development provides a grant or loan of many millions of dollars for forestry projects, the incentives of the forestry agencies and other governmental units to embrace the community forestry elements in these projects are often tremendous. Such projects often include large sums for the salaries of the forestry agency officials involved, vehicles and buildings, international training of forestry personnel, and so on. The chief executive and the financial ministries are usually enthusiastic about the hard currency that such projects bring in. Therefore, if the foreign donors include community forestry components, or if they make government community forestry initiatives part of the requirements for the government to land the project, then community forestry becomes much less of an orphan in government circles.

In Honduras, for example, the national forestry agency COHDEFOR has generally neglected community forestry. It has even been accused of being antagonistic toward community forestry because the communities "get in the way" of the commercial logging that provides the fees that COHDEFOR needs for its operations. Yet funding by the Canadian International Development Agency (CIDA) beginning in 1987 propelled the only significant official project in the Honduran broadleaf forest involving community participation. The broadleaf (hardwood, nonconifer) forests are mixed-species forests that are of little interest to commercial loggers. Given COHDEFOR's dependence on logging fees for its own budget, and the fact that broadleaf forests offer few opportunities to collect sizable logging fees, COHDEFOR has usually shown little interest in these forests. Yet with CIDA providing more than US$3 million of hard currency for the project, it was attractive enough to COHDEFOR for the agency to introduce agroforestry farm systems and forest management conservation with the community playing a significant role. COHDEFOR even moved to revise the stumpage fee system. In contrast to its overall highly negative judgment of Honduran forestry projects, a 1990 Abt Associates assessment for the U.S. Agency for International Development judged the CIDA project as "promising" (Abt 1990d: II–71).

Similarly, the even bigger Olancho Reserve Forest Development Project, begun in 1988 with funding from the U.S. Agency for International Development of over US$7 million, found COHDEFOR quite willing to build in community forestry components and to revamp inappropriate stumpage fee rules (Abt 1990d: II–97). Compare this to the government's own program of Integrated Management Areas (AMIs), which are forest areas of 1,000 to 10,000 hectares under community management for integrated forest uses, each with a resident technician. This program started with modest Food and Agriculture Organization (FAO) support in 1983, but because the state forestry institution COHDEFOR has devoted less than 1 percent of its budget to this initiative, it has had only 2,500 beneficiaries as of around 1990 and in general has functioned poorly. The Abt assessment concluded that because of the limited resources devoted to the AMIs, "It is of little surprise . . . that AMIs have not functioned well" (Abt Associates 1990d: I–13).

Another important means for community organizations to avoid being lost in a politics dominated by larger, more powerful groups is to affiliate with broader movements representing local organizations from other areas. This is well- illustrated by the efforts of Brazilian rubber tappers to convince the national government to establish extractive reserves where the local rubber tappers' cooperatives would be legally protected from attempts by others to cut rubber trees, make counterclaims to the right to tap the trees, or otherwise threaten the viability of the rubber-tapping activities. The government program would also provide funds for the local rubber tappers' cooperatives to buy processing equipment or vehicles to transport the latex.

This was (and remains) a highly contentious issue, because of pressures on the national government and state governments in the Amazon region by ranchers, plantation owners, and large-scale rubber merchants (the so-called rubber barons) to control the same lands. However, toward the end of the administration of President José Sarney (1990), the National Rubber Tappers Council succeeded in getting the federal government to establish the Extractive Reserves Program. The program began to demarcate extractive reserve areas, but only where the government had concluded that competent local cooperatives were already in place. Thus this case also demonstrates that national movements alone, without local activism, would have had dim prospects for success.

Defending existing user rights and restrictions.

The threats to the community's *preexisting* user rights come from all directions. A community can lose its sole right (or its right entirely) if the resource appears to be underused. It is quite common for far-off government officials to overlook existing small-scale forest uses and to conclude that forestlands are truly frontiers. Modest claims are, unfortunately, too often seen as weak claims. The native Dayaks in Kalimantan (Indonesian Borneo) and the Amerindians in Brazil's Amazon have been exploiting their forests for thousands of years, but to the Indonesian and Brazilian governments these areas have often seemed to be uninhabited or sparsely populated wildernesses. Referring to the Amazonian Indians of Ecuador and Colombia, Theodore MacDonald, Jr., (1986: 34) notes, "Land that outsiders perceive as 'idle' (i.e., not put to some obvious economic use) becomes a coveted parcel and an easy target once outsiders learn of its existence." In these circumstances, the government often takes over the jurisdiction of land use in the name of development. In many of these cases, the existing small-scale uses are overridden by larger-scale activities, often undertaken by outsiders.

As mentioned earlier, if governments are interested in providing community user rights, they tend to define community beyond the original user group, preferring instead to endow the rights to everyone within a given geographical or legal unit. Whether the government plans to privatize land or forest resources currently under government control, or to provide access to the entire community, the risk to the original user group is that its own access will be greatly diluted or even eliminated.

Honduras again provides a clear example. The Honduran government has been reconsidering its 1974 action to take over formal control of all trees. For the pine resin tappers, who have been allowed to continue their modest forest uses throughout this period, the new talk of privatization poses a serious threat (Stanley 1991: 30). One fear is that privatization will leave the trees in the hands of wealthy outsiders, who will enclose their land and thereby exclude those engaged in nontimber extractive enterprises. Yet thus far the general policy of the state forestry agency COHDEFOR has presented the opposite problem, by explicitly keeping the access to the resin-tapping areas open to everyone except in unusual circumstances (Stanley 1991: 29). The decline of Honduras's first resin tappers' cooperative, the Cooperativa San Juan, sadly illustrates the problem. Founded in 1966 in the county (*municipio*) of Ojojona, the Cooperativa San Juan started out impressively, growing rapidly from sixty members to over 300 in the late 1970s. Yet by 1991 its membership had fallen to less than thirty-five. The volume of resin gathered by its members has fallen dramatically, reflecting not only reduced effort by the cooperative members but, more significantly, the theft of resin and resin-gathering equipment and the removal of pine trees by outsiders.

This vulnerability reflects both legal and physical conditions. Fencing in the pine trees, or creating other barriers to entry, is not permitted, because the land is formally owned by the *municipio,* which has not been willing to allow the traditional users to exclude others by these physical means. In addition, the cooperative members do not live close to their assigned parcels and therefore cannot monitor the theft of resin and their equipment. Finally, as pine trees in the area have become scarcer due to cutting by outsiders, the competition between resin tapping and other uses of the remaining trees has increased. The vicious circle that leads to deforestation is clearly in play.

Therefore, if a communal organization has to establish a well-defined group of users in order to avoid the logic of over-use, then that organization must enforce exclusion or persuade the government to do so. Several strategies may help to accomplish this.

To prevent the loss of user rights or the loss of exclusivity of user rights, the community needs to legalize and publicize its forest activities. These go hand in hand. Although dealing with the state or national government may be complex, time-consuming, and intimidating, formal recognition may often require launching a project that requires governmental (and often international) involvement. MacDonald (1986) traces the success of the Awa-Coaiquer Indians of the Colombia-Ecuador border. They organized into an alliance of communities headed by an elected governing council. Then they pushed for government recognition of the Awa-Coaiquer Reserve. The importance of pushing the reserve as a development project is emphasized by Macdonald (1986: 34): "In order to prevent confiscation of 'idle' land, a management scheme or 'development' project is essential." The community has to get the government to focus attention on the problem, even though many community units are rather small in terms of the number of people involved. The government must come to realize that these communities have a huge economic, and sometimes also cultural, stake in maintaining their forest access and protecting it from others.

There are three ways to do this. First, it is generally important for the community *to join with higher and higher levels of organization with similar community groups from other areas.* A single cooperative by itself fights an uphill battle against a government interested in the support of more numerous and influential groups or commercial forest exploiters with money, sophisticated strategies, and excellent access to government.

One successful case in Honduras is the Cooperativa Villa Santa–Los Trozos. With the technical assistance of university-educated advisers and lawyers, the cooperative convinced COHDEFOR to grant it a concession to use 22,000 hectares of national forest of highland pines in the mid-1970s, including the rights to harvest and sell the pine trees after their useful resin production years have passed. In this appeal, the cooperative was aided by the national federation of resin tappers, Federación Hondureña de Cooperativas Agro-Forestal (FEHCAFOR), which in the 1980s had more than 2,500 individual members and now numbers more than 3,100 (Stanley 1991: 33). COHDEFOR, in effect, recognized the exclusivity of the cooperative's claim on the area, by intervening to prevent encroachments by outside loggers and others (Stanley 1991: 29). By the early 1990s, most members of the cooperative had inheritable property rights and rights of transfer, which are overseen by the secretary of the cooperative. Members, now numbering around 200, can even engage sharecroppers, who divide the resin yield with the member claiming tapping rights on that particular land parcel. Because they live near their tracts, which are largely fenced in, the tappers can monitor encroachments.

Second, a community group can maintain its exclusion through strategies of physical location. As mentioned, the Villa Santa–Los Trozos cooperative in Honduras benefitted from the physical location of the pine trees close to the homes of the resin tappers. In the short run, the community may not be able to do much about physical locations, except in locating processing facilities among the trees so that community members are at least present during the day during processing seasons. In the long run, however, the planting of new stands may allow for better physical locations.

Third, a community group may have to assign members the responsibility of guarding the resource. Many experiences have shown that policing by the government is often inadequate, and yet if the community does not provide forest guards, then it would be up to the government. This has led to many problems. Sometimes government guards simply withdraw from policing the forest, either because of lack of budget to travel to remote areas, or because government guards prefer the comforts of the cities. In Costa Rica, for example, the staff of the forestry agency receives such a small budget for gasoline that they rarely venture out of the national capital of San José or the provincial capitals (Ascher 1993). Even worse, government guards may turn on the community with arbitrary or heavy-handed control.

Community guards have therefore been emerging in

surprising places. In Bolivia, Indians wrested the rights to nearly two million acres of land in the Beni lowlands from the Bolivian government's original plan (backed by international NGOs) to set up a conservation reserve that excluded the Indians' forest uses. The local organization leaders knew, however, that formal recognition was not enough; they enlisted members of their own group to serve as forest guards. Here again, a community organization cannot expect members to take on this potentially dangerous task without some form of compensation.

There is, of course, an important distinction between the situation of confronting outsiders attempting to exploit the resource and confronting community members (that is, people with recognized user rights) attempting to overexploit the resource. Clashes with outsiders, who do not risk antagonizing their own community members, are generally more serious and more easily escalate to violence. The bloody confrontations between rubber tappers and ranchers in the Brazilian Amazon is a grim reminder of this problem. Unless the community can deter outsiders from using force, it may have to appeal to the government. Yet even if this appeal is made, the community group may still have to maintain a guarding function in order to report violations to the government. In other words, guarding can be useful even if the guards do not have the means or the authority to use violence themselves to chase away the outsiders.

Discipline within the community. We have seen that sustainable management of forests depends, in part, on restraining people outside of the community from exhausting the forest's resources and from reducing whatever capacity for renewability that it might have. But restraining people within the user community is also essential; there is a serious need for internal vigilance. The Honduran resin cooperative of San Juan faced the previously mentioned problem of its inability to guard its trees from outside incursions, but the most devastating blow came when its president stole the equivalent of US$50,000 from its treasury. In Azad Kashmir, a large-scale, government-financed, reforestation program was seriously undermined when the families living around community land, which was eligible for trees planted at government expense, began to partition the land among themselves and treat it as if it were their own private property. In this case the large landowners were more successful in gaining practical (if not legally recognized) control over most of the partitioned land, while the rest of the community became less interested in providing the community cost-sharing because their own potential benefits declined.

Yet internal vigilance is not enough; a community forestry program has to provide sufficient rewards to encourage participation, but at the same time it must require participants to contribute to the common effort and limit the resources that any given participant can exploit. This obviously calls for a delicate balance between responsibilities and rewards. Many cases show that the community's self-restraint requires matching responsibilities with rewards and providing means for resolving disputes.

Matching responsibilities with rewards. The enthusiasm for communal forestry activities is not guaranteed. It requires hard work to plant and care for trees and to guard the resource from others. It even takes hard work to harvest nontimber resources without destroying the resource base. When Guatemalans enter the Petén forests to gather palm fronds (*xate*), for example, their first impulse is to chop as much of each plant as they can, so that they can leave the forest quickly to avoid malarial mosquitoes and poisonous snakes. To conserve the *xate*, however, takes a much more laborious effort of cutting only what is in good enough condition to be exported. To get the same volume of fronds, this strategy requires finding more *xate* plants and more time spent in risky conditions (Dugelby 1992).

The responsibilities required for defending user rights and restrictions include vigilance to guard the resource against encroachment by outsiders and overuse by community members, activism when it is necessary to stand up to the government or other groups, and willingness to make the short-term sacrifice of contributing some profits to the collective enterprise. The

Honduran resin cooperative of Villa Santa–Los Trozos, for example, was successful in building up its financial and administrative capacity because its members were willing to be taxed for each barrel of resin they produced. It had standing with the state forestry agency because the agency saw the cooperative as a well-organized movement that had enough backing from its members to be able to extract financial resources from them. With an economic base of this sort, a cooperative can send representatives to provincial or national capitals, hire whatever experts in law or accounting may be needed, and in many circumstances provide modest payments for forest watchers.

What about rewards? It is essential for community insiders to have clear expectations about the benefits of participating and that these expectations be fulfilled consistently. Consider again the Cooperativa San Juan, cursed with the huge embezzlement and the fact that, because of the theft of resin and resin-tapping equipment, the members' hard work could not translate into higher production. No matter how committed the members were initially to this pioneering cooperative, most drifted away from the communal effort. In contrast, the Cooperativa Villa Santa–Los Trozos, which went through a similar experience of embezzlement by a cooperative leader, overcame that problem because the members of the cooperative retained the expectation that they could still prosper from the cooperative.

The scope of activities of the community organization can play a crucial role in linking responsibilities with rewards. Some activities are risky and costly but do not have direct rewards. For example, the struggles to prevent commercial loggers from encroaching where local people had user rights can be both time-consuming and dangerous. Sustaining community interest would be difficult unless immediate rewards were also available to activists. If a community organization tries to convince people to provide labor for a community woodlot that may take years to reach maturity, or to restrain themselves from tree cutting or hunting, that same organization stands a better chance of gaining their cooperation if it undertakes other projects with short-term benefits. An especially important asset of community groups is their ability to follow up community activism to achieve forest-use rights with the actual community management of the forest resources. Community activism can help to identify people with leadership skills. It can arouse a strong sense of community commitment. In addition, community members need to understand the connections between conservation and economic opportunities; tying them together under the umbrella of a single organization may help to convey that message. For these reasons, *community organizations should try to engage in multiple activities.* Some of these activities can be social or educational rather than economic in nature; the point is to broaden the base of connections that community members have with the organization.

Consider the Indian grassroots movements against commercial logging. The pioneer was the Chipko Andolan (literally the "movement to hug trees"), which began in the central Himalayan region of Uttarakand. It began as a true grassroots movement rather than a nongovernmental organization because local people organized for their own interests, in this case to stop the Forest Department's practice of auctioning upland forestland to commercial loggers, whose operations both reduced available timber and destroyed the watershed. After unusually heavy and destructive flooding in 1970 on the Alakananda River, local villagers began to mobilize. Between 1973 and 1977, the people of the Chamoli district near the Alakananda River protested frequently against the Forest Department's working of the forests. Under the leadership of an inspiring individual, Sunderal Bahuguna,[1] these demonstrations crystallized into the Chipko Movement. The most visible acts of the Chipko Movement have been the open confrontations against the government and commercial loggers. Chipko activists have clung to trees while they were being felled, occasionally leading to severe injuries or death of the activists.

It might seem surprising that people would maintain their enthusiasm for Chipko activism, given this bleak scenario. It becomes clearer, however, when the whole range of Chipko accomplishments is reviewed. First, the protests brought direct, tangible results. The state government of Uttar Pradesh set up a state forest corporation to undertake tree harvesting in some areas without the auction of trees to outside commercial loggers. In other areas, the state government auctioned off the harvesting rights in small-enough parcels for the local people to be able to afford them. Community processing industries were guaranteed supplies of timber, and the state decreed that commercial loggers would have to pay minimum wages to local workers.

Beyond the political battles, though, the movement established an educational mission, teaching the hill people better land use, nursery management, and reforestation methods. Bahuguna also established associated local cooperative societies to exploit timber and nontimber resources without any middlemen. Specific local cooperatives combined political activism, basic economic activity, education, and social activities that are very important in hill communities where large-scale social interaction is difficult. The highly successful Dasholi Gram Swarajya Mandal (DGSM), for example, was based economically on a small woodcraft unit. However, when the government denied the members a quota of ash trees essential for their operations, and instead allotted ash trees from the Mandal forest (only thirteen kilometers from the cooperative) to an Allahabad sporting goods manufacturer, the DGSM launched highly publicized protests against the company. These demonstrations were so successful that by mid-1973 the forest department ended its discriminatory policies on the distribution of forest wood. Forest department officials may have expected that this would end the activism, but the cooperative had already retargeted to challenge the general principle of auctioning to commercial loggers.

After this success, the DGSM established "ecodevelopment" camps in areas seriously affected by landslides and soil erosion in the Alakananda region. Dozens of camps are organized every monsoon and winter season, for educational discussions as well as volunteer tree planting. The five- to ten-day camps, which are open to participation from a wide area and especially encourage women to participate, have a festive atmosphere. The survival rate of the saplings planted by the villagers is over 80 percent and in some cases 95 percent, because villagers take care of the trees collectively. The fodder (which can be produced sustainably after only six months if the forest is properly tended) is fairly distributed among the villagers, according to local custom. The DGSM also provides technical and partial financial assistance for these projects.

Resolving conflicts within the community. Both forest development and forest exploitation involve responsibilities and restrictions on the community itself. Some people will not meet their responsibilities—someone will shirk from weeding the village woodlot, fail to serve guard duty, or plant seedlings without adequate care. Similarly, restrictions will occasionally be violated—someone will get greedy and cut more trees than permitted, or tap someone else's resin. Thus, even when rules and boundaries are clear, conflicts will arise.

Even more serious conflicts will occur when rules and boundaries are not clear, and this is inevitable. No set of rules can handle each and every situation that might arise, no matter how carefully the community organization tries to anticipate them. One part of a forest stand may be destroyed by fire or disease, for example, leaving some forest users without opportunities despite the sacrifices they may have made earlier. They may demand a new deal. Objections may arise to transferring rights through sales or through marriages outside of the community of users. The government may change the user rights or its policies, thereby leading some community members to challenge the fairness of the existing distribution of benefits.

If the community does not handle the bulk of these disputes internally in an impartial and consistent fashion, it becomes vulnerable in several ways. First, if conflicts spill beyond the community, others, including the local area's leaders and the government, may use the conflicts to intervene and either restrict the user group's rights or put outside authorities in charge of exploitation. Since many of the infractions will involve overexploitation, unpunished overuse can easily play into the hands of those who would restrict the user group's general rights to exploit the resource.

Second, unresolved conflicts, or conflicts that appear to be resolved in unfair ways, can destroy the often fragile trust required for community cooperation. Third, decisions that are not considered legitimate by all parties can undermine the validity of further rulings in the eyes of the losers. Fourth, if failures to follow rules or to meet responsibilities go unpunished, the message may spread to others that overexploitation and free riding are possible and that it is foolish for anyone to abide by the rules while others are taking advantage.

For penalties to be enforceable, they have to fairly reflect the seriousness of the violation. If penalties are trivial, they will simply have no force. If penalties are too harsh, then the community itself will not enforce them, or the violators will sever their relationship with the community organization.

Obtaining user rights for state-created resource use opportunities.

From time to time governments create new resource use opportunities. Often, in creating these opportunities the government's intention is to provide a clear-cut benefit in exchange for political support. Therefore governments frequently prefer to offer these privileges to as broad a segment of the area's population as possible. If it has to be selective (for example, in handing out cash, credit, or tax credits for tree planting), the government will often tend to favor wealthier groups whose gratitude may be viewed by the government officials as more politically valuable. Thus when government officials come into a local area with a project to expand the natural resource endowment, they typically grant eligibility to all, with the local leaders in the lead to manage the project and distribute its benefits. Alternatively, the government may simply assign the rights to especially well-connected local business or government leaders.

The distinction between the community of original forest users and the greater community (defined by geographical areas or legal jurisdictions) allows us to appreciate why the community of forest users (that is, people who have been using the forest) so often loses out when elaborate efforts at organizing take place. Forest-users tend to be relatively low-income individuals and families. This is because small-scale harvesting of timber, fuelwood, and nontimber forest products (such as nuts and resins) typically yields much lower earnings than does intensive agriculture or other productive activities—that is why, except when noneconomic reasons prevail, trees remain only on poor soils. These low-income forest users will typically suffer if and when others get involved in exploiting the same forest resources.

Yet when grander plans for forest exploitation begin to be developed, the definition of community is often broadened. Higher-income people take a greater interest in using forest resources; sometimes because of the promise that government money will make forest involvement more lucrative, sometimes because a larger-scale effort can create bigger profit opportunities for people in a position to capture them. Politicians and other powerful local individuals (the local elite) come into the picture, pursuing their own ends or trying to serve the interests of people with political standing—rarely the original poor forest users. Finally, the government, when it is in the position to determine forest-use rights, is usually swayed by considerations of pleasing important political groups; original forest users rarely are among the politically powerful. Since one important objective of collective action in forestry is to strengthen the incomes and security of the traditional forest users, it makes sense to safeguard their rights and the exclusivity of their rights to use the forest.

Often the first task of the user group is to avoid domination of the new project by the local elites. How can a user group stand up to the greater wealth of the local elite? Sometimes, organization can make up for a lack of wealth on the part of the individual members.

The Brazilian rubber tappers' experience shows how governmental action to grant user rights and to increase the economic benefits from resource extraction often go hand in hand. The creation of extractive reserves not only strengthened the rubber tappers' rights to exclusive use of the rubber trees, but also provided investment funds that in some instances have been critical for maintaining Amazonian rubber tapping as an economically sensible undertaking. Where these reserves have been established (albeit very slowly and very few), the Brazilian government has increased the economic benefits in an otherwise very precarious industry, as rubber from plantations in the south of Brazil and imported rubber from Southeast Asia threatened to leave Amazonian rubber without a market.

Original forest users are typically better off if they can organize apart from mobilizing the entire village or broader community, get legal recognition of their exclusive right to exploit the forest resources, and then try to attract any outside help they deem necessary. This sequence is sensible because the original forest users will have an easier time gaining recognition of their special user rights *before* other groups or individuals are made aware of the potential to prosper off of the forest resource. If the government is involved from the beginning, the original forest users must strive to be involved in the planning of expanded forest exploitation, so that the government officials will not slide into assuming that the existing forest is for everyone in the broad area to use.

The importance of this point is clearly demonstrated in comparing two community forestry initiatives in Nepal. Chaap Aal Danda Forest is a small (99.8 hectares) government pine plantation in Nepal's Sindhu Panchlok District. Initially, local people were limited to gathering grass and leaf litter, while seven forest watchers were paid by the government to prevent illegal tree cutting and grazing. No local ownership was acknowledged. In late 1985, twelve years after the plantation was established, several meetings were held at the government's initiative to develop a firewood harvesting plan. The potential forest users (as opposed to the much smaller group of families who had depended on gathering earlier on) were identified as the 544 households of the area, covering three local units (*panchayats*) and many different caste groups. The meetings were widely advertised, yet they were dominated by local politicians. Decisions were made without hearing the opinions of the women and the low-caste people. The management plan was approved for implementation in May 1986, and harvesting began soon thereafter, overseen by an elected forest management team.

The project was plagued by many problems. Information about the harvesting did not reach everyone. The original forest users, who were socially and economically quite distant from the individuals who tended to dominate the district and the meetings, were isolated from the process. With growing animosity and a huge number of families newly entitled to exploit the resource, there was no incentive for anyone to show restraint in removing fuelwood.

The community forestry project for Tukucha Panchayat in the Kabhre Palanchok District also started in 1985, along the same lines as at Chaap Aal Danda. A forest committee formed at the first meeting decided to take responsibility for all the forests in the *panchayat*. In contrast to Chaap Aal Danda, work was started for a much smaller user group, and efforts were made to encourage forest management by the forest users themselves. Initially, the traditional forest users distrusted the government and withheld their cooperation, but as time went on more and more of these people became involved in the program.

Expanding the resource base.

Building up the resource base is in some ways a bigger challenge than maintaining an existing resource base in a sustainable way. Some of the economic principles have already been introduced in Chapters 2 and 3. Here we review some of the organizational challenges and approaches for meeting them. It is important to begin with a distinction between enhancing or expanding an existing resource and creating a new resource base. In the first category we would put programs to reduce extraction so that an existing resource base can recover, tree planting that accompanies tree cutting (often called forest enhancement), introducing additional animals to an area that is already operating as a game or tourist reserve area, etc. The second category would include new village or town woodlots, afforestation of long-denuded or never-forested areas, the creation of a forested game reserve, etc. The distinction is important for two reasons: first, enhancing or expanding a forest resource generally does not raise the issue of user rights, unless the government allows new groups to claim user rights; second, creating a new resource base generally requires big, immediate investments of money and labor, with the bulk of the benefits postponed for several years. Clearly, the creation of new resources presents more complex issues of rights and incentives.

The complexity of this challenge is most clearly shown in the surprisingly poor record of village woodlots. Village woodlots were the great hope of "social forestry"—forestry to involve local people and focus on meeting their needs for fuel, fodder, poles, etc. The World Bank sociologist Michael Cernea wrote, in the mid-1980s, that "[u]ntil recently, the community woodlot has been widely accepted as the dominant model in social forestry." (Cernea 1985: 280). In the 1970s and 1980s, hundreds of thousands of village woodlot efforts were launched in developing countries all over the world. They were very often backed by enthusiasm of the local government; technical assistance and impressive funding by state, provincial, or national governments; and by international agencies. With the technologies of fast-growing tree species, sophisticated nursery and planting techniques, and well-tested watering methods, success might seem guaranteed.

Instead, village woodlots have suffered from severe problems. In many cases, the village provides an inadequate amount of land for the woodlot to be efficient or to provide a significant amount of the village's fuelwood and light-construction needs. Conflicts often arise over the ownership of the land. Conflicts also frequently arise over the distribution of the wood produced and the revenues from harvesting it. [2] Most surprisingly, a huge number of village woodlots have received minimal community participation. One major World Bank–funded initiative was in the Indian states of Gujarat and Uttar Pradesh. Most of the plans for "managed woodlots," for which the forestry department was to do the planting, maintenance, and harvesting, came to fruition. But of the "self-help" woodlots, for which the forestry department was to provide free seedlings and technical advice but the villagers were to be responsible for planting, maintenance, and harvesting, only 43 percent of the target number of woodlots were actually planted and maintained in Gujarat and only 8 percent in Uttar Pradesh (Noronha and Spears 1985: 248). Many of the woodlots designed and launched by forestry departments have remained largely department efforts. After serving as additional chief conservator of forests of Gujarat state in India, S. A. Shah (1988: 62) reluctantly concluded:

At present, creation of village woodlots is a governmental activity in all the states. The development of self-help villages has not, as yet, caught the imagination of the rural community. This fact should not deter the planners in any way, because it is a question of time—maybe 20 years, 50 years or even 100 years before it becomes truly a community effort. The gestation period would depend on how soon the benefits have reached the beneficiaries.

While one can certainly admire Mr. Shah's patience, it is very depressing to think that it might take a hundred years before Indian villagers have an incentive to participate in community tree-growing efforts. What kinds of obstacles stand in the way of greater success in the near term?

Coping with the short time horizons of potential developers. The first difficulty in resource development is the problem of time horizons. Compare this to the basic problem of preventing the overexploitation of existing resources that provide immediate yields to engage the interest of potential exploiters. Initiatives of resource development cannot count on immediate interest because so many forest resources are slow to reach maturity. To build up a resource base, whether through reforestation, community woodlots, or creating facilities for forest-related tourism, people have to invest time and effort now for benefits that may be rather far in the future. Even fast-growing trees seem to grow slowly when the family needs cash to pay for food, medicines, or other pressing needs. Therefore the first challenge of forest-resource development is to generate the commitment and rewards to get people to devote effort that has predominantly long-term benefits.

The fact that expanding the resource base takes significant time to produce benefits means that the particularly low-income members of the user community may not have the resources or patience to wait until the trees have matured sufficiently for sustainable exploitation. Therefore it is important to provide some income-earning opportunities during this crucial start-up period. There are many tasks for poorer members of the community that can earn them something before the resources reach the point at which they should be harvested or otherwise used. Community members are often hired to care for newly planted trees by weeding, thinning, putting up fencing to keep out animals, and guarding the trees against encroachers. They can be given some of the other jobs that a broad-based forest development effort may produce: tourist guides and tourist concession operators, if a tourism component is involved; nursery workers, if an ongoing replanting program exists; and extractors of nontimber resources, if mixed timber and nontimber plants are involved.

The challenge for the community is to provide these funds during the period before the operation becomes self-financing and then to ensure that enough of these job opportunities are available to the poorer segments of the user community, who are at the greatest risk of having to encroach on the timber resources prematurely. Some degree of formal organization is necessary either to collect money from the general community membership in order to pay these wages, or to encourage voluntary labor. Where the strategy is to pay poor members of the user community, an enlightened community organization is essential to convey to other community members why poorer members ought to get these jobs. Indeed, the challenge is made greater because without financing from the government or donors, the community has to provide some of these resources from its own ranks. The community organization's responsibility here is even more important—without leadership, the short-term sacrifice by some community members, and the fact that immediate benefits cannot be equally shared, could cause many community members to back out of supporting the development effort.

The risks of government involvement.   Does it make sense for the organization to seek funding from outside sources, such as the government or international donor organizations? On the positive side, in some cases the participation of the government or other outside institutions, with their capital and expertise, is necessary to launch the initiative. However, government management can squeeze out community involvement.

In the Indian states of Gujarat and Uttar Pradesh, where the World Bank had funded more than 23,000 village woodlot initiatives by 1983, the Bank's assessment concluded that most woodlots managed by the state governments' forestry departments never succeeded in getting significant community involvement and were denied adequate land by the village to establish an efficient woodlot (Noronha and Spears 1985: 248). Now, it may seem strange that a village council and the villagers themselves would turn their backs on a forestry department that provides the bulk of the financial resources and much technical assistance for a joint venture with the village. Mr. Shah provides one answer when he points out that much antagonism has arisen when the woodlot development prohibits the passage of people and livestock through the woodlot area (Shah 1988: 64). Dalvi and Shukla (1988: 45) add that even if the community does become actively involved, cooperative arrangements with the government or other financial sources generally require the profits from forest development initiatives to be shared with the financing institution. In Gujarat state, the revenues from harvesting woodlots involving both village efforts and the Forestry Department are split evenly between the village government (*panchayat*) and the Forestry Department. This may very well be a fair arrangement, considering that the Forestry Department puts in much of the effort and nearly all of the capital, but the *panchayats* that can generate their own financial resources to plant and maintain their woodlots get to keep all the proceeds. [3] In short, the village is losing some of its rights in agreeing to a joint woodlot venture with the government.

The final consideration is that government funding often comes with the requirement that all residents of the geographical area be eligible for involvement in development and exploitation. In some cases this makes little difference, since the land is controlled by the local government on behalf of all people living in the area, so general involvement by anyone in the area who wishes to become involved is a given from the beginning. Yet in other cases the traditional user group that has some claim to the land in question or at least to certain forestry uses on that land may well find that its exclusive user rights become eroded by government policy to include everyone. There is no easy answer to whether it makes sense to try to enlist government or international support and funding for this purpose, but at least the considerations to apply to specific cases are straightforward.

Membership boundaries. Another challenge in organizing for resource development is defining the set of individuals or families to be included in developing the resources and therefore also eligible for the benefits. For programs to create essentially new resource bases, such as planting a new village woodlot or replanting long-denuded hills, defining the community in terms of traditional resource users is not possible. In some cases, the availability of land dictates the answer. If the village commons is the only viable communal land available for the planting of a woodlot, then the ownership by the entire village, and the right of the village government to control it, is already fixed. The challenge in these cases is for the village or town government to provide financing (unless that comes from the government or donors), incentives for the hard labor required to plant and care for the seedlings, policing against premature or excessive exploitation, and the enforcement of principles of fair exploitation. Yet where alternative sites are possible, where land can be purchased or leased by a wide variety of groups, or where several different user groups have customary rights to existing uses of the same land, there are many possibilities for membership. This makes the organizational challenge of resource development fundamentally different from that of other tasks. In one sense this gives tremendous flexibility to leaders who are trying to launch new resource development efforts. But what should be the basis for defining the limits of membership?

According to the logic of individual incentive and group unity, smaller-scale projects, with more limited memberships, have several advantages. Smaller ventures generally provide greater assurance to members that they and their families will actually benefit from the fruits of the venture. A World Bank assessment of many efforts at community woodlots in India and Nepal found that one likely reason why some woodlot initiatives fail is that the eligible population is too large and too diverse (Noronha and Spears 1985: 248). There is a lack of community spirit and shared objectives; a lack of confidence that participation will lead to sufficient rewards. Yet these considerations are often disregarded. For example, Mr. Shah flatly states that as far as woodlots are concerned, "[a] village should be taken as a unit" (Shah 1988: 63). This presumption may be a large part of the problem, insofar as whole villages (especially in a densely populated country like India, where a village may have a population in excess of 10,000 people) are often extremely diverse and populous. The question, therefore, is whether cohesive entities—a small-enough village, a village section, or a related group within the area—can gain access to enough land to make the woodlot worthwhile in the eyes of the involved individuals.

Nurturing and protecting newly developed forest resources. While most of the previously mentioned differences between developing new resources and exploiting established ones point to the greater difficulties in resource development, starting afresh has a few advantages—some design options are more open. Rather than relying strictly on traditional roles, community leaders can try to ensure that all the essential roles are undertaken: nurseries, weeding, guarding, etc. The creation of new forests is, of course, also a particularly opportune moment to plan for easy monitoring. The physical location and compactness of the new plantings, whether woodlots or strip plantations, should be carefully considered so that they can be easily guarded.

Arranging the distribution of benefits. The start-up phase is also the best time to establish how the benefits ought to be shared. There is an important political difference between establishing rules of sharing benefits before the benefits have emerged as opposed to after people have begun to capture them. Before any given household or subgroup knows that it can reap unusually great benefits, it is likely to approve of

117

more equal distributions of the benefits. Once the benefits start to be captured unequally by different people, they naturally tend to lose interest in rules of more equitable sharing. Perhaps this is one reason why forestry cooperation that originates with the user community usually has greater unity than efforts that start with prodding from the outside. The conversations held before the community embarks on expanding the resource base and begins to capture the benefits are less likely to be marked by fights over whether current benefits should be redistributed. In contrast, the moment the government, NGO, or international funder comes into a community that has not yet worked out its sharing plans, the promise of funds can touch off a scramble for special treatment that may well destroy the possibility of cooperation. Thus the Chipko and Appiko movements in India compare favorably with the experiences of Azad Kashmir and Nepal's Chaap Aal Danda, where community cooperation was undermined when outside funding brought out the conflict within the larger community.

Additional purposes of community cooperation in resource development. While much of the preceding discussion focused on community cooperation in the actual joint development of forest resources, such as woodlot efforts, we need to ask whether community cooperation can serve other goals in resource development besides joint development. After all, in many cases community planting does not appear to be very successful, and there are other options that do not involve trying to overcome community divisions: agroforestry or larger-scale plantations on privately held land. Does this mean that community action has little bearing on resource development, as much as it may be important for controlling other aspects of resource use?

On the contrary, there are several other functions involved in resource development for which community cooperation can be very important. First, providing the inputs for tree planting can be a very effective community effort, without the same risks of community divisions and premature cutting, even if the seedlings or saplings are destined for planting on private land. Second, community organization can be instrumental in securing inexpensive inputs (such as planting materials) and technical assistance, whether the planting occurs on communal or private land. Third, community cooperation can be important to mobilize people in the effort to maintain the rights to plant and harvest in particular areas. Fourth, and finally, community organization and discipline in the exploitation of forestry resources and the distribution of their benefits can be very important in determining whether there is the incentive to engage in communal tree-planting efforts. S. A. Shah's insight that villagers are likely to participate only if they see themselves as beneficiaries makes the issue of fair distribution acutely important.

Expanding the processing capacity for existing resource uses.

As mentioned in Chapter 3, the profitability of small-scale forest use sometimes lies as much in what happens after the resource is harvested as in the harvesting. The allure of launching and expanding community processing, both out of optimistic expansiveness and to enhance the power and standing of the organization, can be very great. Chapter 3 argued that these ventures sometimes work well, but they may also lead to disaster.

Thus an essential obligation of the community organization is to undertake a tough-minded analysis of the costs and benefits of any seemingly promising downstream processing or marketing venture. Outside assistance in such a cost-benefit analysis is useful, because of the complexity of business ventures and because community leaders may well lack an objective judgment of their own business skills.

One critical element of this cost-benefit analysis is the analysis of the potential market for the products *as processed* by the community members. Demand is often very sensitive to the perceived quality of the product. Community-processed products are often not as polished, sophisticated, or well-packaged as similar products manufactured by larger-scale, often urban-based producers. Over time, these aspects of quality can and must be improved. In the meantime, a realistic assessment of the true demand for rougher outputs is essential, even though the analysis will not be very popular among the community's enthusiastic backers of the project.

Occasionally, the cost-benefit analysis will reveal that a downstream processing venture would eventually become sufficiently profitable, but lose money until then. If the eventual productivity is high enough to justify forgoing the opportunity to devote the resources to other, more immediately profitable activities, then it is legitimate to support the venture as an infant industry. The questions are whether the community is prepared to increase its efficiency and whether funds are available to cover the losses, pay workers, and continue to invest in the venture. Governments and international donors are sometimes prepared to provide the funding for the promotion of infant industries. All of the risks and pitfalls in dealing with governments hold for this purpose as with the others considered throughout this book.

In those cases where processing and marketing can be an economic success, the community faces even greater challenges of distribution and potential corruption than with the functions of community forestry reviewed previously. Whereas other forms of community cooperation in forestry result in trees and other tangible objects, expanding the processing and marketing capacity results in cash coming in from complicated transactions of investments, loans, payments outside of the community, bank accounts, etc. The need for monitoring is even more important, and yet the results are less visible and the people do not sell their own individual production to people outside of the cooperative. Compare the situation of the Honduran resin tappers before and after the cooperatives came into being. Before, the tappers sold directly to the middlemen. They knew immediately what their gain was, although they often complained bitterly that the middleman was capturing too much of the ultimate profit. With the cooperative arrangement, the individual tappers hand over the resin to the cooperative and only later find out what their net (that is, total) gain or loss will be, even if the cooperative pays them something at the time the resin is brought to the refinery. The obvious point is that the opportunities for cheating by cooperative leaders are much greater. An equally important point is that cooperative members may suspect cheating by the leaders even when they are honest, since expectations of good profits may easily be disappointed because of poor market conditions or costs that are difficult to understand (such as high interest rates on loans).

To address these dangers, it is important for processing and marketing cooperatives to have a management council comprising people who are or can be trained to understand the financial aspects, as well as the physical aspects, of the operation. Many NGOs can be helpful in providing the economic expertise to determine whether a processing venture is actually worthwhile.

The final challenge for processing ventures, assuming that it is worthwhile to go ahead with them, is to preempt the possibility of conflicts over distributing the gains (or losses) once the operation is under way. To address the issue of fair sharing, as with other forms of community cooperation, it is essential to have understandings, before the money starts to come in, as to how to share the gains. Yet it is also essential to come to understandings as to how to cover any losses.

General strategies.

Each of the five functions explored has its own challenge and logic, but there are some general lessons and strategies that cut across all five. It is worthwhile to conclude this chapter by considering these general strategies.

Providing rewards for engaging in collection efforts. The risks and costs of trying to mobilize community action give rise to the first set of design principles related to the need to provide rewards for engaging in collective efforts. It is not reasonable to expect people to engage in the often difficult and dangerous job of community organizing out of sheer goodwill or sense of community responsibility—although in most communities there are a few people willing to make such commitments. Individuals are much more likely to engage in community action if they see some benefit in it for themselves or for others they want to help, whether they be family, clan, neighbors, or others. The individual, or those on whose behalf the individual makes sacrifices, has to receive clear benefits.

Preplanning of community forestry efforts. This calls for preplanning of community forestry efforts *that clearly specifies the expected outcomes of cooperation and how the benefits will be shared.* This holds both for intracommunity efforts (such as the community woodlot) and for efforts that involve others as well. It may seem unnecessary to introduce considerations of greed and selfishness just when community leaders are trying to arouse community cooperation. Yet, especially in poor communities, people generally cannot afford to devote time, money, and effort to activities for which even their share of uncertain gains is unclear.

The second problem arises when many of those who benefit from the efforts of one person do not make any contribution themselves. When others get a free ride, the activist may be discouraged from continuing. Why should he or she continue to make sacrifices so that others can benefit without any costs or risks to themselves? This is the same dilemma that explains why many people do not exert self-discipline in their use of resources when they believe that others will take advantage without making their own sacrifices. This is why all of the functions outlined in this chapter require the community to develop mechanisms to reward effort and to withhold rewards from people who do not contribute.

Keeping organization costs low. While much of the discussion has concentrated on how the community should organize itself to pursue various functions, it is still important to keep in mind that keeping an organization going takes valuable time and effort. A council to oversee the operations of a processing and marketing cooperative may be necessary, but it is equally important to keep the structures simple, so that participation does not become such a heavy burden that community members grow disinterested in participating. As mentioned earlier, one way to economize on effort is to get community organizations to perform several functions.

Another strategy is to make participation as rewarding as possible in itself, for example by mixing social events with organization activities. But the point remains that the costs of participation must be kept within reasonable limits.

Enlisting the help of nongovernmental organizations. The potential for cooperation with nongovernmental organizations has been evident for many of the different kinds of ventures that community forestry may attempt. Nongovernmental organizations can be defined as organizations that have explicit mandates to act on behalf of others, or for broad public goals (such as environmental protection), or both. They are therefore different from the community organizations that we have been examining, in that the community groups are predominantly organized to serve the interests of their own members. The activists and professionals of NGOs are typically from higher educational levels than traditional forest users. They are therefore often better versed in legal and financial issues. Some domestic NGOs are formed by highly successful community activists who are prepared to share their techniques with other communities.

Increasingly, governments and international donors have relied on NGOs to undertake cooperation with forestry communities. Interactions between the community groups and the NGOs frequently involve less friction than relations between the community groups and the government directly.

However, two words of caution are in order. First, NGOs may often be perfectly well-intentioned, but NGO activists, and the people who make their living from working for NGOs, have their own agendas that may not always be the same as those of the forest users. Some NGOs are much more concerned about preserving nature than assisting in the economic development of the area. Some NGO employees are interested in capturing the resources flowing into the area. Second, NGOs sometimes have developed very antagonistic relationships with governments. If forest user communities are seen as allies of these NGOs, the community-government relationship may be in danger. There are, of course, times when the community has to fight to maintain its user rights against the government, and help from such NGOs in the obvious struggle may be necessary. When community groups may have to depend on governmental support, however, the community should be sure to enlist the help of NGOs that are fervent, but not so fervent as to ruin the relationship with the government.

5   Government Support for Forestry Communities

Government officials usually have very mixed feelings about community action in forestry and other areas of natural resource use. Officials tend to be better educated, more worldly, and more exposed to modern ideas than the community members in remote forest areas or in villages appropriate for forestation programs. Therefore many people in government sincerely believe that they are better prepared and better organized to lead a community in forestry activities, or to regulate these activities, than are the members of the community itself. By "community," they usually mean the population of a geographical or legal jurisdiction. Government officials who are conservation-minded often find fault with the local people as selfishly destroying forest resources, for example through game poaching, slash-and-burn agriculture, or overlogging. Government officials who are not so conservation-minded often view local people and their attachment to their land and forests as obstacles. These officials believe that the country needs to develop economically through agriculture, irrigation, industry, hydropower, and mining despite the inconvenience that forests are in the way. In the first of these diagnoses, the community is the problem; in the second, the community is almost ignored.

Increasingly, though, government officials have come to realize that community action can substitute for the expensive need to put government officials into the field. Particularly in terms of forestry, which so often is situated in remote areas, governments can economize on their forestry staff (who often do not want to live or work far from cities anyway) by having communities manage the forests themselves to some degree.

Many government officials have also realized that moving decisions away from national and provincial capitals often leads to better decisions. What local people may lack in education and sophistication is often outweighed by their more intimate knowledge of local conditions: what trees will grow where; what insects or other pests may pose a risk of infestation; why seemingly promising cropland has been left uncultivated.

Yet while governments have become increasingly interested in (or resigned to) decentralizing their own authority over forests and relying on community management, they cannot simply withdraw completely. The basic lesson is that governments must steer between withdrawal and dominance. This is for four reasons.

First, the government is usually the ultimate arbiter of user rights when they are contested beyond the boundaries of single user communities. When a community's claim of forest user rights is challenged or ignored by others, the government often has to decide whether, and how, to intervene in the dispute. When user rights seem to clash and the possibility of violence arises, governments are often obligated to get involved because of their responsibility for keeping public order. Even when governments cling to formal state ownership of land and trees, private individuals frequently use forest resources without formal permission, and the government is often called upon to ratify these uses, often by making them part of a forestry project.

Second, the government is sometimes the only institution strong enough to keep outsiders from encroaching on the rights of established forest users. These forest users are often economically weak and few in number, thus requiring help if powerful outside forces, such as commercial loggers, try to gain control over the forests.

Third, communities cannot always resolve all of their disputes internally—even though it is important that they try to do so to whatever degree is possible. Some disputes have to do with basic issues of rights that are too crucial for either side to give up without a fight—unless the government intervenes to prevent violence. Some issues involve legal interpretations, examination of historical documents such as deeds and intercommunity agreements, and other judicial functions that only the government can perform.

Fourth, in many cases the past neglect of forest resources has left a huge need for investments to restore the resource base. This can be done through obvious means, such as providing seedlings and technical assistance for reforestation, or through more complicated maneuvers, such as establishing forest reserves that allow forests to regenerate while the community is encouraged to cooperate by providing it with income opportunities from tourism, nontimber extraction, etc. For these initiatives to be successful, the government often must finance the operations.

For these reasons, community forestry projects have been a common element of government initiatives in many countries, both where forests still exist and where reforestation has been recognized as desirable. Yet governments often fail in their efforts to promote community forestry. One way to interpret these failures is to assume that government officials may not be serious about giving up their own power. But even when government officials are well-intentioned, their best efforts often go awry. Throughout this chapter, we emphasize that the role of government has to be carefully restrained. There are many temptations for governments to take on roles that are not efficient or effective in government hands. Quite often, doing what seems to be in the interest of a particular forest user group backfires. Governments have assigned user rights to members of a community, only to discover that this action undermines the community's authority to assign the user rights itself. Governments have financed forestry projects, only to find that outsiders force their way in to take advantage of the funds. Governments have taken on the task of policing a forest, only to encounter great hostility from the people in the area that makes effective policing impossible.

To address these pitfalls, this chapter develops some lessons for government officials interested in promoting community forest management. The approach of the chapter is to identify the major dilemmas that face government efforts to deal with community forestry issues and to contrast the designs of more and less successful approaches to dealing with these dilemmas.

Government Dilemmas and Approaches
for Facilitating Community Forestry

The dilemma of conservation versus forest exploitation.

Practically every observer of forestry problems discovers that there are tradeoffs between conservation and forest exploitation. The government is usually held responsible for balancing several objectives: conserving resources for the long term, capturing the riches of the nation's natural resource endowment to put them to use for the country as a whole, and assisting in the development of relatively low-income communities related to forestry. The government must be concerned about ecological damage within the area where people are exploiting forest resources, which risks the sustainability of the forest uses and therefore the long-term incomes of the forest users themselves. Yet the government must also be concerned about the damage to other resources, or to other areas, brought about by forest exploitation: the reduction of nontimber resources (fruits, nuts, resins, latex) by the harvesting of timber; flooding and soil erosion if too many trees are cut; pollution of rivers and lakes from mineral prospecting in forest areas;[1] forest fires that spread from one area to another; etc. Thus two kinds of conservation problems arise: the issue of sustainability (protecting people, and their future generations, from their own actions) and the issue of negative spillover effects (protecting people from the actions of others).

The problem is that the people always seem to be "in the way." Virtually every act to exploit natural resources causes some disturbance to the environment.[2] Therefore it is always possible for the conservation-minded forestry official to point to local people as threats to conservation. Of course, where there are sparse populations, the environment has a better chance to recover. In general, the impact on the resources and the environment depend on population pressures, which affect the degree of resource exploitation by increasing the demand for products made from the resources, increasing the number of people extracting the resources, and often causing migrations of people who are not familiar with how to use the resources without creating significant damage.

This last point makes it clear why it is so important *from a conservation perspective* for the government to uphold local communities' customary user rights. Short of reducing population growth, governments can do little to reduce the demand for products. But the government can limit the number of people extracting the resource, and in particular limit resource extraction to people who have lived in the area long enough to have learned something about conserving the resource for the long run, *by assisting local resource users in maintaining the boundaries against outsiders.*

Another compelling reason for governments to pursue conservation through the recognition of the authority of community organizations is the potential of these organizations (and the general social interaction of the user community) to educate and apply social pressure on community members to treat the resource base responsibly. In terms of both financial resources and manpower, it is much more efficient to rely on social pressure and the penalties applied by a community than to rely on government policing and the formal legal procedures required to enforce governmental regulations. It is also true that government efforts at regulation sometimes unleash such negative reactions from people who view their rights as having been restricted that they may be even less conservation-minded.

Government assistance in limiting forest-use rights to the original forest users can be provided in several ways. The most obvious way is for the government to *assign* the user rights to traditional users. However, we find that this approach holds serious hazards.

It is often thought that the most direct way the government can safeguard the user rights of a forest user community is to sort out the claims to various user rights and ratify some of them as legal. This impulse often begins with a survey or census of past and current uses, with the assumption that established use represents a valid claim for continued user rights. This is quite similar to the role that many governments play in granting legal land titles to farmers. While the fact that the government is paying attention to traditional uses is appropriate, the trap of this approach is that it implies that the government has the legitimate authority to assign these user rights, whether its decisions on who deserves the rights come through its reading of the historical record or by any other means. If this principle is accepted, then the legal standing of the community and its organizations is seriously reduced, for whether or not they are currently receiving the benefit of user rights granted by the government, they have lost the *authority* to assign user rights themselves.

Why is the community's authority to assign user rights so important, even when the government is disposed to grant the rights to that particular community's members? Community authority puts the community organization in the position to *reassign* user rights in the future. Government assignments of user rights, generally as formal, legal, and fixed property rights, lack the flexibility that communities may need to regulate the rate and methods of forest exploitation. Insofar as government assignment freezes user rights to the lucky winners, it denies the community the authority to adjust user rights by its own members as conditions change. Furthermore, when governments assign user rights directly, they deal with the individual or family level, bypassing the community. Thus the government's assignment of user rights elevates private ownership of some members of the community at the cost of other members and at the cost of the community's ability to arrange for the sharing of exploitation opportunities and benefits.

The alternative is clear: *the government should recognize the authority of appropriate forest user organizations to assign and adjust user rights.* For the community to manage forest resources, it has to have the authority to permit, direct, or prohibit forest uses.

In some circumstances, however, the user rights and property rights are confused or indefinite because of competing claims, ownership changes of questionable legality, a lack of community organizations that can assign user rights, or situations in which tenants finally have the opportunity to get secure tenure of farmland with some potential for agroforestry. In these cases, the government faces the difficult choice between trying to encourage the immediate creation of a community organization or government-run titling. If the government takes on the titling task, it should undertake a rapid but careful processing of user-rights claims. In a broad review of countries receiving international support to develop

National Tropical Forestry Action Plans in the 1980s, Larry Lohman and Marcus Colchester found that a consistent weakness of the plans was their failure to provide for government efforts to either recognize or formalize traditional property rights (Lohman and Colchester 1990).

Another important but subtle way that the government can uphold existing user rights is to make it clear that it will not grant benefits of government forestry projects to large landowners or other powerful local people who present shaky claims to land or forest user rights. It must be remembered that government activism in forestry often has the unfortunate and ironic effect of attracting wealthy and powerful people to claim user rights at the expense of the existing, low-income forest users. In Azad Kashmir, for example, the Pakistani government established the Hill Farming Technical Development Project, which included a large component of fuelwood planting on 7,500 hectares of "community-owned land" (*shamilat* land), which had a total expanse of over 800,000 hectares. Small farmers were expected to be the main beneficiaries of the project. However, the government failed to enforce the community property status of the *shamilat* land as large farmers informally asserted their control over parts of this land in order to qualify for free trees planted at government expense. If the government had made it clear at the outset that it would carefully monitor whether community land would continue to be used by the community rather than by private individuals, the temptation for large landowners to assert their control would have been much lower.

However, it is generally a huge mistake for governments to go one step further and prohibit forest uses by anyone. With the exception of small areas of particularly important or delicate ecosystems, prohibiting forest uses simply does not work. As explained in Chapter 4, forests are generally too large and too remote for government officers to police effectively without spending far more than governments are willing to pay. At first glance it seems easier to ban whole categories of forest uses (such as tree cutting or hunting) altogether than to allow for some of these activities, but traditional forest users who have depended on extracting some income from the forests will usually continue, with great animosity toward the government and far less reason to be concerned about the forest's sustainability. Once outsiders see that the traditional forest users have lost their exclusive rights, and yet the government cannot prevent violations, the outsiders often move in.

In spite of the seemingly proenvironment image of sweeping prohibitions on forest uses, they are seldom effective and often counterproductive. In Liberia, for example, the Forestry Development Administration was required to enforce a law in the 1980s imposing a total ban on hunting in Liberian forests, despite the fact that game provides an indispensable 80 percent of the rural population's animal protein (ITTO 1988: 48). As mentioned in Chapter 4, the Pakistani authorities had to contend with 50,000 cited violations within the Azad Kashmir area at one time in the late 1970s. Once people are forced by necessity to defy government regulations, it becomes less compelling for them to obey other regulations. Impossible regulations also provoke the kinds of confrontations that destroy the trust between communities and government.

Similar restraint is necessary in determining the appropriate penalties that the government should impose for violating forestry restrictions. Just as there is a temptation to try to enact sweeping bans, it is tempting to try to frighten people into obeying the rules by imposing very harsh punishments for rather modest infractions. This is also generally counterproductive, since excessive punishments reduce the likelihood that other people will report violations. Heavy punishments, whether fines, imprisonment, or confiscation of property, also motivate people caught in such violations to try to bribe government officials. In addition, an overly punitive government can easily destroy whatever trust may have existed between the community and the authorities.

A principle for limiting the government's conservation role.   So far we have presented reasons for and against a prominent government role in conservation of forest resources. Is there a broad principle that can guide the government's decisions as to when to assert its power? One crucial consideration is that some forest exploitation causes damage that goes beyond the forest user group. If this damage is not borne by the users who cause it, there is little chance that they will be motivated to reduce the damage. *The need to address these spillover effects, [3] if they are serious enough, justifies government action on behalf of the wider society.* On the other hand, environmental damage that directly affects the interests of the forest users ought to be addressed by the users' community. For the government to take over this task, it would have to presume that it knows what is good for the forest users better than the forest users do themselves.

This distinction between damage borne by the community and damage beyond the community raises again the important question of how the limits of the forest users' community are to be defined. Yet it is this very distinction that helps define the boundaries. A community is defined by common interest—it consists of people who have enough regard for one another, or who interact so closely with one another, that a positive or negative impact on one part of the community is similarly felt by the rest of the community. Thus there are natural boundaries of potential communities as defined by common interests. Insofar as community organizations actually reflect these boundaries, both the government and the community organizations will find rather clear distinctions between internal impacts and spillover effects. For example, the reduction of *xate* palms gathered exclusively by a particular *xatero* community in Guatemala's Petén region will be felt by the entire community, but the presence or absence of *xate* is virtually irrelevant to anyone else. Therefore it should be up to the community to decide on the rules for restraining *xate* gathering. In contrast, the actions of a community with tree-harvesting rights can easily have impacts beyond the community if the loss of trees means the destruction of a watershed serving other people as well. The soil erosion and flooding that might result from the disappearance of the trees thus becomes a legitimate concern for governmental action.

But how should the government deal with such cases, if the reality is that any resource use is likely to cause some damage, even if very minor, to someone else? In the situation of land where community groups have substantial user rights, we surely do not want governments to feel compelled to strip away forest users' rights by asserting state ownership; nor do we want them to engage in heavy-handed regulation whenever there are such spillover effects.

In terms of the government's budget, the least costly way to deal with this problem is to make the damage-causing community aware of the damage (perhaps by arranging joint meetings with the communities suffering damage, as long as such meetings would not result in uncontrollable conflict), and, if the damage continues, tax the damage-causing community the equivalent of the economic value of the damage. As it is difficult to gauge the value of the damage, and communities may be tempted to continue damaging activities secretly, a more effective if more expensive approach is to provide subsidies to encourage pollution-reducing and degradation-reducing practices. In other words, the government can redefine the challenge from preventing damage to encouraging positive spillover effects; for example, rewarding watershed protection as a service to the public good rather than punishing communities for damaging the watershed. As discussed later in this chapter, it is important for the government to avoid making these subsidies so high that they attract efforts by the community group and outsiders to take advantage of the subsidies in exaggerated and counterproductive ways.

For land currently under state ownership, the government has the option of leasing forestland to community groups for specific uses. For many years, governments have granted leases (so-called concessions) to commercial loggers, often with requirements to adhere to environmental standards. Although concessions have rarely been revoked because of environmental violations, revocations have occurred. Granting long-term leases to community groups rather than to commercial loggers also has the potential to pressure community groups into obeying environmental regulations through the threat of revoking the lease. If granted to community groups, leases would fall between granting permanent user rights and retaining state control.

The challenge is to design lease conditions that come close to being regarded by community members as indefinite user rights, so that the forest users will care deeply about the long-term survival of their area of the forest system, while still perceiving a risk to their rights if they cause damage to other areas or to other communities of users. This requires granting long-enough leasing periods, such as the ninety-nine–year periods now granted in the Philippines. It also requires environmental regulations that are reasonable and free of political manipulation. The danger is that if community groups come to believe that leases are insecure because of the possibility of political manipulation, the forest users may well come to believe that rapid exploitation is the sensible approach because they may lose the lease even if they try to comply with environmental conditions.

Another option for state-controlled land is to merge government forestry efforts with community efforts, in order to turn potential enemies into allies. Since 1980, for example, strip plantations on state-owned land in the Indian state of Gujarat (along highways, canals, railroad tracks, etc.) are planted by the state forestry department, but protected by nearby villagers. These watchmen are paid to monitor ten hectares of plantation area for the first year and twenty hectares for the next two years. The harvest revenues are shared equally between the village *panchayats* and the government of Gujarat. For village woodlots established by the Forest Department for those villages incapable of undertaking their own (for lack of finances or other reasons), the control is handed over to the village after three years, and, when harvested, a fifty-fifty split of proceeds is made. Nontimber resources, such as deadwood, fruits, etc., can be removed by anyone (Dalvi and Shukla 1988: 44–45, 68).

The dilemma of small-scale exploitation versus development.

Many governments have traditionally viewed standing forests as obstacles to development. While large-scale commercial logging may produce financial windfalls as decades of tree growth are cashed in all at once, the standing forest appears to be a forgone opportunity for massive logging, agriculture, grazing, or other apparently higher-yielding activities. The people living in and near the forest, who are using it in various low-intensity ways, are thus viewed as contributing little to development. There has been much recent rethinking of this shortsighted view. The newer view is that forestland has remained forest largely because it cannot sustain other, more ambitious uses; that low-intensity use may be the only sustainable use; and that forests serve crucial but less obvious purposes, such as watershed protection and climate moderation. Nevertheless, many governments still operate under doctrines based on the idea that a forest is a wilderness representing a lack of development. In the Philippines, for example, the so-called Regalian Doctrine, dating back to a Spanish decree of 1897, declares all land not covered by official land titles to be owned by the state. Forestland populated by people living off of forest products could be taken over by the government for more intensive purposes (Halpin 1990: 15). In Costa Rica, forests are sometimes referred to as *tierra sucia*—"dirty land." Title to forestland can be obtained by demonstrating that it has been "improved," which can be accomplished by cutting down the trees.

This mentality poses three dangers for community forestry. First, it implies that traditional forest uses as practiced by local forest users do not have high-enough yields. Second, it implies that state control over forest resources, already justified in the minds of some government officials as a means of *conserving* natural forests, is favored by other officials as a means of *converting* natural forests into farms, pastures, and plantations. No wonder governments over the years have assumed so much control over forestlands, despite their usual inability to administer these lands effectively. Third, it implies that community organization is a further obstacle to progress, because organized communities can fend off government development initiatives more effectively than can individuals acting alone.

The existence of these attitudes goes far in explaining why there is so much mistrust between governments and forest-using communities. While we can assume that many government officials no longer hold these attitudes, even such enlightened officials must recognize that a large part of their task has to be to overcome this image. Some of the most successful efforts by governments to assist in community forestry are therefore modest, unobtrusive efforts that do not raise the fear that the government is using its programs to take control.

The government of Haiti, where the mistrust between the people and the government has traditionally been as great as in any other country, was very successful in its Agroforestry Outreach Project begun in the early 1980s (Rhodes 1990; Murray 1984). After many previous disappointments with government interventions, the Agroforestry Outreach Project simply established seedling nurseries and trained agroforestry extension agents to work with NGOs, church organizations, community groups, and individuals to stimulate interest in tree planting on private farmland, which in Haiti is typically divided into very small, family-owned farms. Through the 1980s, this program (funded largely by international donors) delivered more than 50 million trees to more than 200,000 farmers. Conflict was minimal, because there were no challenges to customary user rights.

Many government officials have also looked to forest products as a promising avenue of industrialization. The idea is for the domestic economy to capture all of the gains from producing the expensive, finished product. For countries endowed with a natural resource such as timber, there is often the belief that processing it within the country into more expensive finished products (such as furniture) would bring great economic benefits. This strategy has been especially attractive when there are possibilities for exporting the finished goods; that way the country can earn foreign exchange.

This strategy has been shown to have serious weaknesses. Finished products should indeed sell for more than their raw inputs, but that does not mean that the additional revenues from selling finished products are adequate in terms of the investments required. In many cases, bigger profits could be earned by simply exporting the raw materials and using these earnings along with available labor to pursue more productive economic ventures. It is also true that many countries produce these finished goods much less efficiently than the few established leading producer countries (Vincent and Binkley 1992). The Honduran state forest-products industry, which concentrated on exporting pine building supplies, collapsed because other countries have more efficient sawmills (Miranda et al. 1992). Indonesia produces a lot of plywood, but because the Japanese produce it more efficiently, the Indonesian manufacturers can be competitive only by getting hidden government subsidies to keep down the costs of the plywood manufacturers (Gillis 1988a: 107). Finally, the very existence of the industry often leads to rapid exhaustion of the timber supply needed for the industry to survive in the long run. Several countries famous for their timber, such as Costa Rica and Indonesia, have already encountered serious supply shortages that have required the shutdown of expensive processing facilities.

Despite these flaws in the strategy, however, many governments persist in thinking that a forest-products industry is a good idea, and that large-scale commercial logging companies can supply the timber more rapidly and more efficiently. It is generally true that they can supply the timber more rapidly—that is one reason why supplies are being depleted—but their greater efficiency is highly questionable. With bulldozers, heavy trucks, and no particular affection for any piece of land, commercial loggers often cause tremendous damage to the forest near each tree that they harvest. Yet until this inefficiency is recognized by government officials, governments will continue to award logging rights to commercial companies as part of the supply strategy for forest-products industrialization. This is especially common when the same companies that process timber also request the rights to cut the trees for their own supply.

This emphasis on commercial logging and promoting the domestic forest-products industry has three negative effects on small-scale forest users. First, logging rights are often given to these commercial companies even if the community had prior user rights. When this happens, the commercial loggers are often given the further right to prevent local people from even extracting nontimber resources. Not only does commercial logging destroy many trees suitable for resin tapping, rubber tapping, and fruit and nut gathering, but local people may be prevented from entering land that has virtually been made the temporary property of the commercial loggers.

Second, to force loggers to offer timber for domestic production at affordable prices, many governments have banned the export of raw logs. This hurts the small-scale loggers even if they were not cutting trees for export, since in general the local prices for timber will go down. When the Indonesian government banned the export of whole logs, the loggers, both large and small, lost out because of the rapid drop in log prices. This drop occurred because the ban eliminated the foreign market, and domestic sawmills were therefore able to buy the logs much more cheaply (Gillis 1988a: 71).

Third, communities that organize themselves to fight for their user rights end up locked in confrontation not only with the companies, but also with the government that awarded the logging rights to the commercial loggers. The tendency of governments to look upon commercial logging as part of their country's push toward modernization compels small-scale forest users either to give up or to challenge the government. In these confrontations the community groups are put in a bad light because they seem to be obstructing national economic progress. The government and the commercial loggers look bad because they are suppressing the rights of the poor and marginal. Any nongovernmental organizations that come to the aid of the community also end up in conflict with the government, a situation that very well may close off opportunities for cooperation among the government, the community, and the nongovernmental organizations.

There is one simple lesson to all of this. Government officials should not assume that forest-products industries and commercial logging are necessarily good for the country. While there must be some countries where domestic production of finished wood-based products makes sense, governments must consider the prospects carefully before unleashing the damage to community forest uses that the combination of forest industry and commercial logging would create.

Even when the government recognizes that community forest users ought to be part of the forestry effort, there are often differences in interests that cause conflict between the forestry officials and the community. The forestry officials typically wish to get the maximum timber production. Therefore, when the government provides financing for tree planting, it usually pressures the communities to plant as much as possible in conventional plantation fashion. For example, the Indian foresters Vishwa Ballabh and N. C. Saxena (1991: 7) note that huge targets (an afforestation target of 5 million hectares annually announced by the then Prime Minister in 1985 meant planting on an average 24,000 trees in each village of India every year) forced the Forest Department to adopt strategies of inducing farmers to do high density plantations, rather than to popularise low input tree cropping which would produce more grasses and complementary agriculture.

However, as easy as it may be for government officials to think of local people involved in forest uses as forest users, even people who are much more reliant on the forests than others are only part-time forest users. Except for some employees of commercial logging companies, people use the forests to supplement their incomes from other activities, usually farming, fishing, or both. Communities would often much rather mix trees and agricultural crops on their land and keep the time that has to be devoted to forest maintenance low enough to allow them to tend to their other income opportunities as well. This may reduce the government's capacity to feed the forest-products industry, but without community enthusiasm the production of trees is likely to be even lower. Obviously, for the government to kindle the enthusiasm of local communities, *it should support multipurpose rural development programs rather than try to impose a straight plantation plan onto people who want and need more diverse activities.*

The dilemma of the degree of government control.

When government officials wish to promote new activities involving low-income people, these officials often view themselves as the agents of change and the people as resistant to development. Sometimes this is reinforced by a tendency on the part of the officials to lump together all the people of a forested area, only to conclude that many people are uninterested in organizing for forestry activities (without a lot of government money thrown in). The lumping together may make the government officials lose sight of the fact that many people within a geographical area may not have customary rights to forest use or a need to exploit the forest. However, their disinterest does not mean that forest users are uninterested or resistant to change in principle.

When forest users are indeed resistant to government-promoted change, the reasons are more likely to be suspiciousness and sensible economics than laziness and ignorance. The suspiciousness of government actions arises directly from the common experience of governments taking over user rights and then blaming local people for the overexploitation that results from the government's inability to enforce restrictions on forest use. Government officials must cope with the suspicion that government action so often arouses even if their motives are straightforward and honorable. Most governments have to overcome the legacy of past government actions that stripped user rights away from local people.

In the Philippines, for example, forestry officials are bewildered by the seemingly irrational actions of the Ifugao people to burn forests for agriculture despite a "high level of tree-consciousness" even among the slash-and-burn cultivators (Diaz 1982: 117). The foresters' evaluations of attitudes among the Ifugao center on their ignorance: "The majority are not aware of the negative consequences of burning which they accordingly intentionally resort to due to shared beliefs that forest burning would increase soil fertility and enhance the growth of forage for animals" (Diaz 1982: 117). Of course, forest burning does increase soil fertility in the short run. For a slash-and-burn cultivator with other land options after a few crops are raised on burned land, this short-run fertility is sufficient. The long-term fertility is more the problem of the government than the cultivator in relatively low population areas.

The other finding about the Ifugao is more illuminating. Forestry researcher Celso Diaz reports:

It was also shown how the government through its implementing arm played a role in the perpetuation of forest burning. . . . It was discovered that the tendency to burn a forest appears to be born out of a socio-cultural and political climate whereby the governmental relationship with the local people surfaces as a major issue. . . . [The shifting cultivators] perceive that forestry laws are ineffective due to non-implementation and consequently show a very low regard for government authorities. . . . They are very wary of government-sponsored programmes and the tendency of some is to openly negate what the forestry agency is out to do. (Diaz 1982: 117–18)

A similar pattern is seen in parts of India. Forest users have reacted to remarkably patronizing attitudes of forestry officials. P. N. Gupta of the Uttar Pradesh Forest Department wrote the following:

The story of rights and concessions is old and complex and even the British rulers accepted the position as too difficult to change. The existing rights make it extremely difficult to manage the forests efficiently. (Gupta 1982)

Gupta then goes on to list the complicated government classifications imposed on the rights to harvest various types of trees since 1877, including some areas where all rights to cut trees were eliminated ("old reserves" where only grazing, grass cutting, and leaf plucking were allowed), others requiring the permission of the magistrate to cut prized tree species that the government declared as protected, others restricting the harvest even of nonprotected trees. The new awareness of today might have led Mr. Gupta to recognize that the government's own action of placing these trees off-limits to people who had customary rights, and the government's ineffectiveness in upholding the restrictions, were responsible at least in part for the deforestation by both people who previously had customary rights and those who did not. His view, instead, was that the government was both well-meaning and competent; the local people were the culprits:

To further meet the requirements and needs of the local people, there were protected forests, known as civil forests in Kumaon, and these were managed by the Revenue Authorities for the benefit of the people. Similar forests in erstwhile Tehri Garhwal State . . . are known as Soyam forests. At one time the condition of these forests was also like that of the reserved forests but most of these forests have been destroyed by uncontrolled exploitation by the village people. (Gupta 1982: 69)

His general conclusion is that the fault lies with the people:

The administration problem is that it is the common belief that forests are gifts of Nature for the unrestricted use of the people. Any restrictions imposed for the protection of the forests are considered to be a forfeiture of their natural rights. (Gupta 1982: 68)

It is important to note that Mr. Gupta did not distinguish between "village people" and the very specific castes, clans, or families that had prior rights to exploit the forests in question. He also saw the actions of forest users to protect or restore their rights as agitation.[4] Is it any wonder that the forest users were leery when the Forest Department came with an offer to help them?

The reluctance to embrace government programs also often comes from the sensible economics that local people apply in judging whether government projects should be embraced. Government officials have to realize that community members are not passive subjects who will (or ought to) do everything the government suggests, but rather are businesspeople. As Chapters 2 and 3 demonstrate, the right combination of income and security is necessary for people to find reforestation projects worth their time, effort, or income. Similarly, government conservation plans often limit the income opportunities of forest users, at least in the short term, which low-income people can ill afford. And if the forest users suspect that conservation measures will be ineffective because of the government's inability to enforce them against outsiders, or that the government may change the policies in the future, then even the long-run gains of conservation may be doubted.

Because many government officials have not recognized these sensible reservations that local people often have toward government initiatives, these officials frequently conclude that it is necessary for the government to impose community forestry onto the people. Put this way, the approach is revealed as a fundamental contradiction. Usually government officials disposed to creating participatory programs in forestry even when the local people are unenthusiastic would put it differently; they would say that they are creating institutions to kindle a spirit of participation that otherwise would be lacking. However, this optimistic perspective ignores two problems.

First, the programs may not be to the liking of the local people, in which case the government will probably be blamed for their failure. The government is caught in a bind: it may wish to create programs involving participation, but programs run by the government very often discourage enthusiastic participation. This occurs because community members want to control their own affairs, and government-created programs are frequently seen as disguised attempts at government control. The lack of cooperation in village woodlot initiatives reviewed in Chapter 4 is a clear example.

In fact, participatory groups often already exist, but they are practically invisible to government officials sitting in the national or provincial capital. As noted in Chapter 4, the informal cooperation among forest users to work together in exploiting the resource (for example, the expeditions of Guatemalan frond gatherers into dangerous forests), expand the resource base, or share the costs of processing are usually quiet, unassuming activities. The forest users' cooperation to defend or restore their user rights may grab more attention, but then the forest users may be labeled as dangerous agitators.

Second, the government may be tempted to create institutions for participation that are, nonetheless, essentially controlled by the government. Trying too hard to establish community forestry can result in the creation of artificial, government-controlled institutions that do not capture the loyalty of the community, or institutions that are eventually spurned by the government when they try to assert their independence.

A good example of the ineffectiveness of government-controlled "community" organizations is found in the Mexican state of Oaxaca. In the late 1970s, several community groups in Oaxaca formed the Organization in Defense of Natural Resources and Rural Development in Sierra Juarez (ODRENASIJ). Similar to local efforts in other states, ODRENASIJ fought the extension of long-term concessions to private firms in hopes of winning local access to forests. When the concessions ended in 1981, there was no formal policy response by the national or state governments. In 1982 the president issued a decree that renewed the private concessions. However, in 1983, communities in the Sierra Juarez and throughout Mexico finally gained control of their forests.

When the concessions policy ended, communities in Oaxaca became responsible for their forest resources. Most communities had no experience in forestry management and few financial resources. Although ODRENASIJ officially disbanded after the concessions ended, a few experts in the group continued to provide advice to the communities. Even so, while the communities had access to their land, they lacked money, organization, and the technical expertise to manage their resources effectively. The communities also faced increasing competition in the timber market and increasing demands for individual access to the forests. By 1988, many independent community organizations had formed throughout the state of Oaxaca, but the state government's unresponsiveness to their claims for recognition and for the exclusion of commercial loggers led these organizations to try to form larger organizations. After a year and a half of frustration, twelve communities tried to form a permanent union. However, the state government, trying to promote its own statewide umbrella organization, ARIC-Forestal,[5] blocked this initiative. The state government had, and still has, the authority to deny the legal registry of cooperatives. The state government only allowed three smaller cooperatives to be formed and pressured them to join ARIC-Forestal. Two of these cooperatives, comprising seven communities, soon joined ARIC-Forestal, thus becoming official cooperatives under the control of the state government.

These official cooperatives have encountered serious problems. The distribution of profits is decided by the state officials, resulting in a decline of cooperation by community members. For the communities enmeshed in ARIC-Forestal, deforestation remained a problem, and community participation in joint efforts such as reforestation was weak. In 1992, the state effort collapsed.

Some groupings of communities managed to avoid being incorporated by the state government. The Unión Zapoteca Chinanteca de la Sierra Juarez (UZACHI), established in 1989, was formed by the other five communities, situated in the Ixtlan region of the Sierra Norte of Oaxaca, that were not absorbed within the ARIC-Forestal official organization. UZACHI's problem was that it did not yet have official, legal recognition. Other community forestry organizations, such as Unión de Comunidades y Ejidos Forestales de Oaxaca (UCEFO), already had legal recognition and were able to operate effectively despite the pressures of ARIC-Forestal to join the state organization (Madrid 1993). Yet UZACHI had to organize its communities to petition for recognition from the same state government that controlled the rival ARIC-Forestal. Essentially, these communities simply resisted the pressure to join ARIC-Forestal long enough to see the state organization decline. When ARIC-Forestal was disbanded in 1992, UZACHI finally received official recognition. The political nature of legal recognition could not be clearer than in this case.

Since then, UZACHI has taken good advantage of its legal recognition to coordinate the efforts of the five communities. From the beginning, UZACHI implemented plans to stem the deterioration of forests and to improve the communities' standard of living. In community meetings, the members of the five *ejidos* of UZACHI decide how profits from commercial activities should be spent on behalf of the community, for example on health centers, churches, public buildings, irrigation systems, agricultural machinery, and wheat mills (Bray 1991).

In forestry, UZACHI has reformed the harvesting practices that were used under the government-owned paper and pulp company that previously held the forest concession. The government company had been removing only the very best trees ("high-grading"); UZACHI began selective harvesting that includes removing malformed and diseased trees and leaving high-quality seed trees (Bray 1991: 23). Because of its importance as a source of income to the communities, the forests controlled by UZACHI are well-protected by the communities. Individual access to the forests is restricted in a way similar to what had been done by the private firms. However, because the local people benefit from community production, illegal cutting and selling of wood has not been a problem. While some areas have limited felling and foraging, other areas are not cut or exploited at all. Land designated for forest use is no longer cleared for agricultural use. The UZACHI communities work together in setting up programs and implementing policies that protect aquifers, restore areas damaged by fire, and set aside reserves for long-term growth (Bray 1991).

A more complicated example comes from Costa Rica, where the government often channels financial support from international donors into local communities through NGOs. Because these NGOs are, by definition, outside of the government and seem to represent "activism," many government officials and international donors operate on the assumption that the NGOs' involvement either fulfills the need for local participation or would somehow ensure that such participation would actually occur among local people. In the Talamanca region of southeastern Costa Rica, forest conservation activities are coordinated by a host of governmental organizations, including the National Parks Service, the General Forestry Directorate, the Wildlife Office, the National Commission on Indigenous Affairs, and the Ministry of Mines, Energy, and Natural Resources. In addition, the Asociación de los Nuevos Alquimistas (ANAI), a Costa Rican environmental group, has worked in the Talamanca region since 1976. Its efforts are concentrated in the Gandoca-Manzanillo Wildlife Refuge and the La Amistad Biosphere Reserve.

ANAI's development and conservation activities have focused on establishing clear land tenure for small-scale farmers, sound ecological practices, and market diversity. ANAI sponsored a new category of land in protected areas. Under the program, small-scale farmers were allowed private ownership of the land, but had to comply with restrictions on use in the protected areas. Farmers were assisted by ANAI in completing the complex process of gaining title. ANAI has also sponsored several programs to promote agroforestry and agricultural development, promoted a local cacao marketing cooperative, and introduced tropical fruit trees as an alternative crop. Forty communities have now established self-supporting tree nurseries, with 1.8 million trees having been planted. Small research projects on agroforestry and plant species are designed to help farmers maintain agricultural plots in the forests. A community technician program educates local leaders in agricultural development. The program has attracted the support of the national government for both conservation and development in the area.

This record seems quite impressive, but it is the result of nearly US$1.5 million of spending by private donors, foundations, NGOs, and a Dutch debt-for-nature swap. ANAI rates its own efforts as successful (McClarney 1989: 42); however, ANAI's projects have been criticized by outside consultants as being sporadic and too dispersed to indicate clear positive results for conservation. Though ANAI stresses its ties with the area, local participation has been limited. With the exception of the marketing group, local organization has been insignificant and formal local involvement in decision making has been lacking. Relations between ANAI and the communities have suffered because local groups see ANAI's conservation efforts as depriving the area of opportunities for large-scale development. ANAI's reputation has also been damaged by bureaucratic difficulties, such as delays by the government in granting land titles (Wells and Brandon 1992).

As argued in Chapter 4, nongovernmental organizations can be very useful bridges between government and communities, and they can often provide needed technical assistance more efficiently and cheaply than the government directly. However, the Costa Rican example, and the general principle that people make greater commitments to endeavors of their own making, call for the government to avoid relying exclusively on the NGOs. They also call on the government to choose NGOs that have their own commitment to encouraging genuine community activism, rather than relying on NGOs that simply want to implement projects themselves without bothering to involve the local people except when absolutely necessary. To its credit, ANAI did have a commitment to promoting community activism, even if it was not as successful in achieving this objective as it may have wished.

Thus the efforts of government to promote community forestry require self-restraint on the part of government officials. It is important to try to encourage communities to organize themselves, but not to fill the vacuum with overbearing government programs, outside NGOs lacking support of the communities, or artificial community groups that are really creatures of the government. Government officials have to avoid both the arrogance of ignoring local communities and the arrogance of overcontrolling community activities.

If community groups cannot function well as creatures of the government, then it follows that *community groups must be allowed by the government to organize independently.* A very plausible explanation for why forest users often seem reluctant to form community groups is their worry that the government would be hostile to independent organizations.

In many countries, independent organization still requires government recognition, because groups must have legal standing in order to own property, apply for loans, hire employees, or run an office. Yet this official recognition is very different from governmental control that would give the government power to select or veto a group's leaders, place a government official as chair of the cooperative's board, or otherwise insert the government into the operation and decision making of the community group.

This point may seem obvious, but in practice it is often a challenge to maintain the boundary between community groups and governmental entities. In Honduras, for example, the program to establish Integrated Management Areas (AMIs) was conceived as a way of getting communities involved in forestry management, with technical assistance provided by government employees. The government handed over to the AMIs some responsibilities to supervise forest uses. Yet the AMIs are designated to cover specific geographical areas; they have been delegated governmental functions, such as forest use regulation; and they are official elements of the national government's forestry plans and projects. In other words, the Honduran government did not simply recognize forest users' rights to organize, it involved them in new state institutions. And because each AMI covers a geographical area, it is responsible for representing the interests of all within that area, rather than the possibly distinct interests of various types of forest users who may wish to organize independently.

If the government needs to recognize, nurture, and interact with forest user groups without controlling them, how can it do so without arousing suspicion that it is maneuvering to dominate? The contrast between the Chaap Aal Danda and Tukucha community forestry initiatives in Nepal (first introduced in Chapter 4) illustrates what may be necessary to overcome this suspicion. In both cases the local people did not initially understand or trust the intentions of the government and the project officers, leading to lack of cooperation and even obstruction. However, in the Tukucha Panchayat, the deliberate process of consulting with community members and the involvement of forest users in developing the project outline went far in reassuring the local community that the government was neither trying to trick forest users into losing what little rights they had before, nor imposing an unrealistic plan developed by bureaucrats in the capital. The preparation of a forest management plan was to be done within the village itself. There was no time constraint put on the development of this plan, so the villagers had time to understand what was involved and required in forest management. Local enthusiasm—and improved forest management—emerged once the people of Tukucha Panchayat settled on a forest management plan.

The problem-plagued Chaap Aal Danda Forest project, in contrast, was a rushed affair, launched after the government convened a few meetings. Adequate levels of trust and understanding were never reached, in part because a plan was quickly finalized, largely with the ideas of the government officials and project officers from outside of the area.

Another way the government can exercise self-restraint is simply to offer seedlings or other tree-planting inputs (such as planting tools) to communities or individual households without any further incentives and without any further obligations on those who receive the inputs. Sometimes it is even convenient to do this indirectly through NGOs. Community members who are leery of entering into any agreement with the government that obliges them to plant particular types or numbers of trees, or to harvest or sell their trees in particular ways, may be quite willing to accept opportunities to plant on individual or communal land with their own labor as long as there are no strings attached. Recall the Haitian Agroforestry Outreach Project: with the simple act of the government offering seedlings and advice, more than 40 percent of the trees survived. Compare this to the far lower survival rates in countries such as Costa Rica, where reforestation incentive schemes have offered lucrative tax credits that are captured by individuals and companies (often with no forestry experience) who plant vast numbers of the cheapest types of trees and then put minimal effort into caring for them (Ascher 1993).

The final issue of the scope of government control concerns technical assistance. In some respects, technical assistance is the most useful input that government can provide. When the community group is trying to extend processing capacity, technical assistance is useful for steering the community through the problems of dealing with unfamiliar aspects of marketing, processing, and finance. Government assistance, even if it is not to control the operation, can also help to keep community leaders honest in their handling of community finances. Technical assistance is also very helpful for the introduction of new technologies. But the most dramatic need for technical assistance arises when recent migrants begin to exploit the forest or the land that surrounds the forests. Migrants, whether coming into the area on their own or through government resettlement programs, usually have the greatest deficits in understanding the forest harvesting techniques and agricultural practices appropriate for local conditions. Government forestry officials with long local experience can be instrumental in helping these migrants avoid unsustainable practices.

However, the technical assistance mentality carries a risk that the government officials will come to believe that they have the answers and the local people are ignorant. Successful resource exploitation, whether in forestry or other activities such as agriculture or fishing, requires a *balance* of local knowledge and modern science and economics. Communities that have lived in particular areas for long periods have invaluable knowledge about local conditions that may be wasted if outsiders bring in other forestry systems (such as exotic tree species unfamiliar to the local people) or prohibit existing practices without fully understanding their rationales. India's Appiko Movement, for example, was more successful than the government's reforestation programs in the hill districts of Karnataka State in promoting tree planting because the government relied on exotic (that is, non-native) tree species that the local people found to be too risky to plant as well as too expensive. In Gujarat state, the government's afforestation program lacked enthusiastic support because although the government offered planting materials and a monthly cash payment lasting for fifteen years, the people recognized that a single-species forest, unlike the mixed forests they had developed themselves, could not provide the diversified income possibilities that they required.

Governments must also recognize that extension services, the most common form of providing technical assistance, often have serious problems. Underpaid extension agents sometimes go into business for themselves in selling fertilizer, pesticides, chain saws, and other products that create a conflict of interest in the advice they give to the people. Extension agents in agriculture are sometimes hostile toward forestry, either because they view the expansion of agriculture as their mission, or because they see bigger markets for themselves as agriculture spreads into forestlands.

The dilemma of equity.

In dealing with small-scale, grassroots issues such as community participation in forestry, government officials have often been put into a very difficult position on the question of whether the community is everyone within an area or specific groups. For several decades after World War II, government officials were told that "development" meant knitting together the entire nation under the leadership of a strong, central government that could overcome regional, ethnic, tribal, religious, and other differences. Then government officials were told that local participation is essential, and that decentralization is important both to put people's fate back into their own hands and to allow for more competent policies that take local conditions into account. Therefore many efforts have recently been launched to give more power to local authorities.

This reliance on the existing local leaders came about because it is often hard for government officials to keep in mind that the people who most heavily rely on using the forest are typically the poorer, marginal families in the geographical area. The geographical area or administrative district does not contain one big, happy family in which everyone looks out for everyone else, but rather a whole set of different classes, castes, clans, ethnic groups, or other divisions that have typically been competing with one another over resources for decades or even centuries. When authority is put into the hands of the area's leaders, whether they are formal leaders (for example, mayors or village council heads) or informal leaders because of their prestige and political-economic power, the low-income forest users are not necessarily well-represented or well-served. When it comes to natural resource management, and especially to decisions on who has access to resources, giving power to local officials or to the most influential local people often results in a weakened position for the poorest people.

This is particularly serious for the maintenance of existing forest user rights, because small-scale forest exploitation (as opposed to commercial plantations or commercial logging of vast stands of natural forest) usually provides rather low income levels that are unattractive to the better-off in the area, until the government starts to pour in resources. The dilemma, then, is how government can allow for local participation without playing into the hands of the local elite.

The answer is that there are quite different kinds of local participation, hinging on the different definitions of "community" discussed in Chapter 4. If community is defined as the existing forest users, then the chances of control falling into the hands of the local area's most powerful people are much lower than if community is defined as all people within a geographical area.

This is again illustrated by the ill-fated Chaap Aal Danda

initiative in Nepal. The government's rushed overture was to the entire district—project officials convened a few, area-wide meetings that were therefore dominated by the district's most powerful individuals. The project staff made a number of naive assumptions. First, they assumed that the district had one cohesive local community, with clear boundaries from other geographically defined communities. This falsely implied that the local community and the local forest users were the same. Second, they assumed that public meetings open to all would give everyone an equal chance to express their interests, yet low-caste individuals and women (both categories having been firewood gatherers) were given little opportunity to express their views. Third, they assumed that the forest committee chosen at the meeting (again, largely notables from the area rather than customary forest users) would reflect all interests fairly. The traditional forest users viewed this as a threat, because their customary rights were being diluted by the government's decision to extend them out to far more households.

In contrast, for the Tukucha forestry initiative the Nepalese government spent much more time consulting with forest users before formulating a process for developing a forestry plan. There were frequent and informal visitations by project and Forest Department staff to collect data and identify problems. Focus group discussions were held with the forest users to hear their opinions, particularly those from women and low-caste people. In the course of these consultations, officials discovered that specific families were forest users, that access rights were complicated, and that any project could easily create conflicts over access rights and border disputes unless the users were given an adequate role in the mechanisms for resolving disputes. Instead of closeting themselves with a few area leaders to formulate a plan, the government convened larger meetings to elect a forest management committee. The duties and responsibilities of the committee members were also determined at these meetings.

This reorientation was part of a more general reform in Nepal that redefined the "community management unit" from the *panchayat* (village unit) to the "forest users' group." These forest user groups were delegated ownership authority over forest resources (Rhodes 1990: 20).

*The dilemma of agency autonomy and avoiding
fragmentation of policy making.*

Everyone who favors greater efforts at community forestry or
forest conservation talks about the need for a strong forestry
agency that can assert the importance of its mission against
other priorities represented by other government agencies.
They often talk about the need for a forestry agency with as
much independence as possible and with as high a status
within the government as possible. The dilemma is that a
forestry agency that charts a strong, independent course
may neglect the crucial need to coordinate with other government agencies that affect community forestry in often un-
foreseen ways. The impact of government efforts in forestry
come not just from the direct projects that everyone labels as
forestry projects or forestry programs, but also from a host of
other policies that are not necessarily identified as related to
forestry. The problem that emerges is that these various
policies, programs, and projects are often developed apart
from one another. The result may be that well-intentioned
forestry programs and projects are undermined by other policies that were not developed with these programs and projects in mind.

First, many government policies have nonobvious impacts
on the markets for the products made by community forestry
efforts. An overvalued foreign exchange rate will make it less
profitable for harvesters of exportable products such as pine
resin, nuts, or latex; for every dollar of export earnings, the
harvesters and processors receive a smaller sum in local currency to divide. The general availability of credit and the fairness of access to credit for low-income individuals and groups
is also very important, as mentioned in Chapter 3.

Second, population settlement programs in particular can
do enormous damage to community forestry, and yet the policy
makers who decide on these programs are often surprisingly
insulated from the impacts of these programs. The damage occurs because the combination of greater population pressure
and government grants of land-use rights to the new settlers
undermine existing user rights. The settlers' ignorance of local
conditions often contributes to overexploitation and unsustainable forestry practices. Clashes between the original

people and the newcomers can also destroy any sense of unity of the larger community.

If the government does persist in relying on resettlement programs into forested areas, it has an obligation to make thorough studies of the target area to ensure that the land selected for agriculture and other purposes can sustain the migrant population and to provide sufficient technical assistance to the migrants to train them in sustainable forestry and agricultural practices. In resettlement schemes ranging from India to Indonesia to Brazil, major problems are found in government's failure to do adequate studies of soils, pests, weather patterns, water problems, and so on. People are typically brought in with inadequate preparation for the local conditions that they will face (Ascher and Healy 1990: Chapter 4).

Third, the defenders of forests against other land uses often clash within government. In Costa Rica, for example, officials in ministries promoting agriculture and ranching have often seen forestry (and the General Directorate of Forestry) as being in the way of progress. This has even extended down to noticeable conflicts between agricultural extension agents and forestry officials. Often this conflict could be resolved if the highest government officials supported the definitive use of one land classification system to determine land uses across the country. Without this top-level decision, different government agencies will adopt the land-classification system most convenient for their own expansion and influence. In both Costa Rica and Indonesia several very different land classification systems are currently in effect, making for considerable confusion and often resulting in the destruction of forests by private individuals—migrants, farmers, ranchers—who have the support or at least the tolerance of some government officials (Ascher 1993).

A similar confrontation was found in India over the issue of agroforestry, clearly an area requiring cooperation between the agricultural and forestry agencies. Vishwa Ballabh and N. C. Saxena (1991: 7) note:

The discipline of agro-forestry has been ignored till recently by both Agriculture and Forest Departments of the government, because of a tradition of competition for land between the two departments. Each department has a target to fulfil, and hence mono-cropping to the exclusion of intercropping is preferred by both the departments.

Without cooperation among different government agencies, particularly forestry and agricultural agencies, the government cannot expect much cooperation from local communities caught between conflicting government initiatives.

Notes

Chapter 1

1. Specifically, the weighted average of the reduction in forest and woodland from 1977–1979 to 1987–1989, according to World Resources Institute 1992.

2. It is not a coincidence that minerals are so often found in forest areas: high mineral concentrations in soils tend to render them unsuitable for agriculture.

3. In economics, these are called "negative externalities."

Chapter 2

1. Ethiopia provides an extreme example. In 1974 Ethiopia's revolutionary government declared a drastic land reform that stripped an enormous amount of land away from the absentee landlords, the military, and the church. The land was "given" to poor agricultural workers, many of whom had been working the land for the absentee landowners. These new small-scale farmers were at first very enthusiastic about their "ownership" of the land. However, the government also required that the bulk of the farmers' produce be sold to the government's own food agency, at prices set by the government. Therefore the government controlled the incomes of the farmers, regardless of their formal ownership of the land. Because the farmers did not have the right to sell their produce on the open market, their ownership was not very meaningful in terms of the income they could count on. In other words, the assurance of *profitable* future use was lacking.

2. Many people have tried to make a distinction between "legal" (de jure), and customary or actual (de facto) property and use rules. This is quite misleading because it implies that in order to make de facto and de jure rights consistent, those who establish and enact the laws, i.e., the government, have the authority to "legalize" de facto or customary rules. In addition, complementary, overlapping, or conflicting de jure and de facto rights sometimes exist within a single resource area, and both governments and

resource users vary in their ability to enforce use restrictions. The source of authority for customary use rights may come from deeply held community views of the forest resource, as well as from government policy or legislation. Governments, community groups, and individuals sometimes have tremendous latitude in both interpreting and reforming user rights.

3. There are some exceptions. In most countries, the minerals under the soil are considered the property of the state, regardless of the ownership status of the land. In some countries, the government has claimed ownership of trees, regardless of the land ownership.

4. Garrett Hardin (1968) condemned communal property in a very influential essay that implied that communally held land would be overexploited because access was open to the community or even beyond the community of traditional users. In calling this "the tragedy of the commons," he created a stigma against communal property and a tilt in favor of private and state property that is still a serious bias in many places. The "tragedy of the commons" is really a critique of open-access resources rather than communally held and *communally controlled* resources.

5. For useful discussion of *panchayats* see Agrawal 1994.

6. For details concerning this pattern in Colombia, see Miranda et. al. 1992: 277; for India, see Fernandes et. al. 1988: 306; for Indonesia, see Hurst 1990; for Mexico, see Bray 1991 and Bray et. al. 1993.

7. Wilson and Thompson (1993: 299) note that *ejido* lands "are 30%–50% less productive than comparable private farms and represent, according to some Mexican analysts, an opportunity for increased productivity through privatization."

8. Often called "negative externalities" by economists, because the effects are "external" to the people whose actions cause the damage.

Chapter 3

1. These issues are discussed thoroughly in Hazell, Pomareda, and Valdés 1986.

2. As opposed to agent middlemen, who negotiate the transfer of ownership from the seller to the buyer, usually for a commission from one or the other, or both (Desai 1984: 238)

3. These are called "autonomous" rubber tappers as distinct from the "captive" tappers who pay rent to "patrons" and are often permanently indebted to the patrons as their source of credit for market goods. Fortunately, the autonomous arrangement is becoming more common while the captive arrangement is declining (Allegretti 1990: 255–56).

4. Largely a species called *acai* palm (*Euterpe precatoria* Mart.).

5. Stanley (1991: 31) reports that by the 1990s there were three resin processing companies in Honduras, but that they had formed a (legal) cartel, called the Resin Fund, to fix the price of resin purchased from the tappers.

6. The publications on agroforestry are now quite numerous. Good reviews and collections of cases include Nair 1989 and 1992 and Anderson 1990; many fine technical and sociological articles appear in the journal *Agroforestry Systems*.

7. Kanowski and Savill (1992: 376) note the "widespread occurrence of certain macro- and micronutrient deficiencies, notably phosphoros and boron."

8. Some of the findings in Central America are summarized in Wille 1990.

9. Castro (1988: 42–43) lists only the honey gathering as a conservation risk, due to the practice of starting fires to smoke out the bees.

10. For Mexico, see Gomez-Pompa and Kaus 1990; for India, see Shah 1988; for Malaysia, see Gillis 1988b: 135.

11. Even if moneylenders are technically permitted to operate, government restrictions on the interest rates they are allowed to charge can effectively drive them out of business, or at least force them to conduct business illegally.

12. For example, studies of Malawi (Bolnick 1992) and Pakistan (Aleem 1990) find cases in which moneylenders make profits consistently above their costs, with the default risk being minimal because of careful screening, social pressure, or recourse to legal action. Studies of Thailand (Siamwalla 1990) and India (Iqbal 1988) reveal some cases of moneylenders' charges reflecting the costs and risks with only modest profits. Some studies show that even within the same area there is a wide variation in interest rates, depending on the economic circumstances of the borrower and the nature of the loan contract (Iqbal 1988; Sarap 1991). The vast research on this topic is summarized in the World Bank's *World Development Report 1990*.

13. Many of these problems are summarized in Adams, Graham, and Von Pischke 1984.

14. Buying only a partial share of the harvest or the proceeds makes more sense than buying it all, since the developer still needs an incentive to exploit the resource successfully.

Chapter 4

1. A conservator of forests for the Tehri-Garhwal District has said of Bahuguna that "he and the Chipko Movement have achieved more in 10 years than the forestry department could have done in 100 years."

2. Surveys of the record and problems of community woodlots can be found in Cernea 1985, Shah 1988, Noronha and Spears 1985, and Rao 1984.

3. Dalvi and Shukla 1988: 45. Excellent information on these initiatives can be found in this book and in Noronha and Spears 1985.

Chapter 5

1. In many countries, unregulated mineral prospecting relies heavily on the use of mercury, with significant health risks.

2. There is a fashionable myth that the original, native populations in particular areas are somehow in harmony with their environments, or at least were before outsiders interfered with them. The truth is that people of all types exploit resources in ways that change the environment. For example, before Europeans arrived in North America the original forests of the Great Plains states had been eliminated, largely by fires that were probably set deliberately.

3. In the economics literature, these are labeled "negative externalities." See Pearce and Turner 1990.

4. "People have always been agitating for relaxing of restrictions and wanting extension of their rights and concessions" (Gupta 1982: 68).

5. Asociación Rural de Interés Colectivo de Comunidades Forestales de Oaxaca (the Oaxaca Rural Collective Association of Forestry Communities).

References

Abt Associates. 1990a. *Belize Natural Resource Policy Inventory.* USAID/ROCAP RENARM Project, Technical Report No. 110, Vol. II. October. Bethesda, Md.

———. 1990b. El Salvador Natural Resource Policy Inventory. USAID/ROCAP RENARM Project, Technical Report No. 113, Vols. I-II. August. Bethesda, Md.

———. 1990c. Guatemala Natural Resource Policy Inventory. USAID/ROCAP RENARM Project, Technical Report No. 113, Vol. II. April. Bethesda, Md.

———. 1990d. Honduras Natural Resource Policy Inventory. USAID/ROCAP RENARM Project, Technical Report No. 111, Vol. I. May. Bethesda, Md.

Adams, Dale, Douglas Graham, and J. Von Pischke, eds. 1984. *Undermining Rural Development with Cheap Credit.* Boulder, Colo.: Westview Press.

Agarwal, B. 1986. *Cold Hearths and Barren Slopes.* London: Zed Books.

Agarwal, Arun. 1994. "Rules, Rule Making, and Rule Breaking: Examining the Fit between Rule Systems and Resource Use." in Elinor Ostrum, Roy Gardner, and James Walker, eds., *Rules, Games, and Common-Pool Resources.* Ann Arbor, Mich. The University of Michigan Press.

Alcorn, J. B. 1989. "An Economic Analysis of Huastec Mayan Forest Management." In *Fragile Land of Latin America: Strategies for Sustainable Development,* ed. J. O. Browder. Boulder, Colo.: Westview Press.

Aleem, Irfan. 1990. "Imperfect Information, Screening, and the Costs of Informal Lending: A Study of a Rural Credit Market in Pakistan." *World Bank Economic Review* 4 (3) (September): 329–49.

Allegretti, Mary. 1990. "Extractive Reserves: An Alternative for Reconciling Development and Environmental Conservation in Amazonia." In *Alternatives to Deforestation: Steps toward Sustainable Use of the Amazon Rain Forest,* ed. Anthony Anderson. New York: Columbia University Press.

Anderson, A., and M. Jardim. 1989. "Costs and Benefits of Floodplain Forest Management by Rural Inhabitants in the Amazon Estuary: A Case

Study of Acai Palm Production." In *Fragile Land of Latin America: Strategies for Sustainable Development,* ed. J. O. Browder. Boulder, Colo.: Westview Press.

Anderson, Anthony, ed. 1990. *Alternatives to Deforestation: Steps Toward Sustainable Use of the Amazon Rain Forest.* New York, NY. Columbia University Press.

Anderson, E. N. 1992. "Can Ejidos Work?" Paper presented at the 1992 Common Property Conference in Washington, D.C.

Ascher, William. 1993. "Science and Forestry Policy in Costa Rica and Honduras." Duke University Center for Tropical Conservation Working Paper. May. Durham, N.C.: Duke University.

Ascher, William, and Robert Healy. 1990. *Natural Resource Policymaking in Developing Countries.* Durham, N.C.: Duke University Press.

Ballabh, Vishwa, and N. C. Saxena. 1991. "Farm Forestry—A Review of Issues and Prospects." Institute of Rural Management, Anand, India. Manuscript.

Bates, Robert. 1988. "Governments and Agricultural Markets in Africa." In *Toward a Political Economy of Development,* ed. Robert Bates. Berkeley: University of California Press.

Bolnick, Bruce. 1992. "Moneylenders and Informal Financial Markets in Malawi." *World Development* 20 (1): 57–68.

Bray, David. 1991. "The Struggle for the Forest: Conservation and Development in the Sierra Juarez." *Grassroots Development* 15 (3): 12–25.

Bray, David, Marcelo Carreon, Leticia Merino, and Victoria Santos. 1993. "On the Road to Sustainable Forestry." *Cultural Survival Quarterly* 17 (1): 38–42.

Browder, John. 1988. "Public Policy and Deforestation in the Brazilian Amazon." In *Public Policies and the Misuse of Forest Resources,* ed. Robert Repetto and Malcolm Gillis. Cambridge: Cambridge University Press.

———. 1990. "Extractive Reserves Will Not Save Tropics." *BioScience* 40: 626.

Castro, Alfonso Peter. 1988. "Southern Mount Kenya and Colonial Forest Conflicts." In *World Deforestation in the Twentieth Century,* ed. John Richards and Richard Tucker. Durham, N.C.: Duke University Press.

Cernea, Michael. 1985. "Alternative Units of Social Organization Sustaining Afforestation Strategies." In *Putting People First: Sociological Variables in Rural Development,* ed. Michael Cernea. New York: Oxford University Press.

Clay, Jason. 1988. *Indigenous Peoples and Tropical Forests: Models of Land Use and Management from Latin America.* Cambridge, Mass.: Cultural Survival, Inc.

Colchester, Marcus. 1986. "Unity and Diversity: Indonesian Policy towards Tribal Peoples." *The Ecologist* 16: 89–98.

Dalvi, M. K., and Rohit Shukla. 1988. *Evaluation of Gujarat Social Forestry Programme*. Ahmedabad: Sardar Patel Institute of Economic and Social Research.

Desai, Vasant. 1984. *Issues in Agriculture and Forestry*. Bombay: Himalaya Publishing House.

Diaz, Celso. 1982. "Socio-Economic Thrusts in an Integrated Forest Management System: The Philippine Case." In *Socio-economic Effects and Constraints in Tropical Forest Management*, ed. E. G. Hallsworth. Chichester: John Wiley and Sons.

Donner, Wolf. 1987. *Land Use and the Environment in Indonesia*. Honolulu: University of Hawaii Press.

Dugelby, Barbara. 1992. "Getting the Goods out of the Woods." *International Ag-Sieve* 5 (1): 4–5.

Food and Agriculture Organization. 1993. *Forest Resources Assessment 1990: Tropical Countries*. Rome. FAO.

Fearnside, Phillip. 1983. "Land Use Trends in the Brazilian Amazon Region as Factors in Accelerating Deforestation." *Environmental Conservation* 10 (2): 141–48.

Feeny, David. 1988. "Agricultural Expansion and Forest Depletion in Thailand 1900–1975." In *World Deforestation in the Twentieth Century*, ed. John Richards and Richard Tucker. Durham, N.C.: Duke University Press.

Fernandes, Walter, Geeta Menon, and Philip Viegas. 1988. *Forests, Environment and Tribal Economy: Deforestation, Impoverishment and Marginalisation in Orissa*. New Delhi: Indian Social Institute.

Gillis, Malcolm. 1988a. "Indonesia, Public Policies, Resource Management, and the Tropical Forest." In *Public Policies and the Misuse of Forest Resources*, ed. Robert Repetto and Malcolm Gillis. Cambridge: Cambridge University Press.

———. 1988b. "Malaysia: Public Policies and the Tropical Forest." In *Public Policies and the Misuse of Forest Resources*, ed. Robert Repetto and Malcolm Gillis. Cambridge: Cambridge University Press.

Gomez-Pompa, A., and A. Kaus. 1990. "Traditional Management of Tropical Forests in Mexico." In *Alternatives to Deforestation: Steps toward Sustainable Use of the Amazon Rain Forest*, ed. A. Anderson. New York: Columbia University Press.

Gregersen, Hans. 1988. "Village Forestry Development in the Republic of Korea: A Case Study." In *Whose Trees? Proprietary Dimensions of Forestry*, ed. Louise Fortmann and John W. Bruce. Boulder, Colo.: Westview Press.

Gupta, P. N. 1982. "The Effects of Government Policy in Forest Management in the Himalayan and Siwalik Region of Uttar Pradesh, India." In *Socio-economic Effects and Constraints in Tropical Forest Management*, ed. E. G. Hallsworth. Chichester: John Wiley and Sons.

Halpin, Elizabeth. 1990. "Indigenous Peoples and the Tropical Forestry Action Plan." June. Washington, D.C.: World Resources Institute. Manuscript.

Hardin, Garrett. 1968. "The Tragedy of the Commons." *Science* 162: 1243–48.

Hazell, Peter, Carlos Pomareda, and Alberto Valdés, eds. 1986. *Crop Insurance for Agricultural Development: Issues and Experience.* The Johns Hopkins University Press. Baltimore.

Hurst, Philip. 1990. *Rainforest Politics: Ecological Destruction in South-East Asia.* London: Zed Books.

Iqbal, Farrukh. 1988. "The Determinants of Moneylender Interest Rates: Evidence from Rural India." *Journal of Development Studies* 24 (3) (April): 364–78.

ITTO (International Tropical Timber Organization). 1988. "Liberia." *Pre-Project Report.* Vol. II. London: International Institute for Environment and Development.

Jones, Jeffrey. 1988. "Socio-Cultural Constraints in Working with Small Farmers in Forestry: Case of Land Tenure in Honduras." In *Whose Trees? Proprietary Dimensions of Forestry,* ed. Louise Fortmann and John W. Bruce. Boulder, Colo.: Westview Press.

Kanowski, P. J., and P. S. Savill. 1992. "Plantation Forestry." In *Managing the World's Forests,* ed. Narendra Sharma. Dubuque, Iowa: Kendall/ Hunt Publishing Company for the World Bank.

Lasswell, Harold D. 1936. *Politics: Who Gets What, When and How.* New York: McGraw-Hill.

Lohman, Larry, and Marcus Colchester. 1990. "Paved with Good Intentions: TFAP's Road to Oblivion." *The Ecologist* 20, (3) (May–June): 91–98.

Lutz, Ernst, and Hermany Daly. 1990. "Incentives, Regulations, and Sustainable Land Use in Costa Rica." World Bank Environmental Working Paper No. 34. July. Washington, D.C: World Bank.

MacDonald, Theodore, Jr. 1986. "Anticipating *Colonos* and Cattle in Ecuador and Colombia." *Cultural Survival Quarterly* 10 (2): 33–36.

———. 1992. "From Reaction to Planning: An Indigenous Response to Deforestation and Cattle Raising." In *Development or Destruction: the Conversion of Tropical Forest to Pasture in Latin America,* ed. Theodore Downing, Susanna B. Hecht, Henry Pearson, and Carmen Garcia-Downing. Boulder, Colo.: Westview Press.

Madrid, Sergio. 1993. "UZACHI of Sierra Juarez, Oaxaca." Mexico City: Ford Foundation. Manuscript.

McKean, Margaret. 1982. "The Japanese Experience with Scarcity: Management of Traditional Commons Lands." *Environmental Review* 6: 63–88.

———. 1993. "Management of Traditional Commons Land (Iriaichi) in Japan." In *Making the Commons Work*, ed. Daniel Bromley. San Francisco: ICS Press.

McLarney, Bill. 1989 "ANAI: Idealism Survives in the Humid Tropics; Nonprofit Costa Rican Environmental Group." *Whole Earth Review* (62): 44–47.

Miranda, Marie Lynn, Olga Corrales, Michael Regan, and William Ascher. 1992. "Forestry Institutions." In *Managing the World's Forests*, ed. Narendra Sharma. Dubuque, Iowa: Kendall/Hunt Publishing Company for the World Bank.

Murray, Gerald. 1984. "The Wood Tree as a Peasant Cash-Crop: An Anthropological Strategy for the Domestication of Energy." In *Haiti Today and Tomorrow: An Interdisciplinary Study*, ed. Charles Foster and Albert Valdman. Lanham, Md.: University Press of America.

Nair, P.K.R., ed. 1989. *Agroforestry Systems in the Tropics*. Dordrecht: Kluwer Scientific Publishers.

———. 1992. "Agroforestry Systems Design: An Ecozone Approach." In *Managing the World's Forests*, ed. Narendra Sharma. Dubuque, Iowa: Kendall/Hunt Publishing Company for the World Bank.

Noronha, Raymond, and John Spears. 1985. "Sociological Variables in Forestry Project Design." In *Putting People First: Sociological Variables in Rural Development*, ed. Michael Cernea. New York: Oxford University Press.

Pearce, David W. and R. Kerry Turner. 1990. *Economics of Natural Resources and the Environment*. Baltimore, Md. The Johns Hopkins University Press.

Peters, C. M., A. H. Gentry, and R. O. Mendelsohn. 1989. "Valuation of an Amazonian Rain Forest." *Nature* 339: 655–56.

Puetz, Detlev, and Joachim von Braun. 1991. "Parallel Markets and the Rural Poor in a West African Setting." In *Markets in Developing Countries: Parallel, Fragmented, and Black*, ed. Michael Roemer and Christopher Jones. San Francisco: ICS Press.

Rao, Y. S. 1984. *Community Forestry: Some Aspects*. United Nations Development Program, East-West Center, and Food and Agriculture Organization. Bangkok.

Rhodes, William Stacy. 1990. "The Role of the State and Donor Organizations in National Forestry Policy and Programs: A Comparison of Haiti and Nepal." Durham, N.C.: Duke University Center for International Development Research. Manuscript.

Roemer, Michael, and Christopher Jones. 1991. "The Behavior of Parallel Markets in Developing Countries." In *Markets in Developing Countries: Parallel, Fragmented, and Black*, ed. Michael Roemer and Christopher Jones. San Francisco: ICS Press.

Salafsky, Nick, Barbara Dugelby, and John Terborgh. 1993. "Can Extractive Reserves Save the Rain Forest? An Ecological and Socioeconomic Comparison of Nontimber Forest Product Extraction Systems in Peten, Guatemala, and West Kalimantan, Indonesia," *Conservation Biology* 7 (1) (March): 39–52.

Sarap, Kailas. 1991. "Collateral and Other Forms of Guarantee in Rural Credit Markets: Evidence from Eastern India." *Indian Economic Review* (2) (July–December): 167–88.

Schwarz, Adam. 1989. "Timber Troubles," *Far Eastern Economic Review*, April 6: 86–88.

———. 1990. "A Saw Point for Ecology," *Far Eastern Economic Review*, April 19: 60.

———. 1992. "Trade for Trees." *Far Eastern Economic Review*. June 4: 61.

Schwarz, Adam, and Jonathan Friedland. 1992. "Green Fingers: Indonesia's Prajogo Proves that Money Grows on Trees." *Far Eastern Economic Review*. March 12: 42–44.

Shah, S. A. 1988. *Forestry for People*. New Delhi. Indian Council of Agricultural Research.

Siamwalla, Ammar. 1990. "The Thai Rural Credit System: Public Subsidies, Private Information, and Segmented Markets." *World Bank Economic Review* 4 (3) (September): 271–95.

Stanley, Denise. 1991. "Demystifying the Tragedy of the Commons," *Grassroots Development* 15 (3): 27–35.

Tucker, Richard. 1988. "The British Empire and India's Forest Resources: The Timberlands of Assam and Kumaon, 1914–1950." In *World Deforestation in the Twentieth Century*, ed. John Richards and Richard Tucker. Durham, N.C.: Duke University Press.

Turner, S. D. 1988. "Land and Trees in Lesotho." In *Whose Trees? Proprietary Dimensions in Forestry*, ed. Louise Fortmann and John W. Bruce. Boulder, Colo.: Westview Press.

Vincent, Jeffrey, and Clark Binkley. 1992. "Forest-Based Industrialization: A Dynamic View." In *Managing the World's Forests*, ed. Narendra Sharma. Dubuque, Iowa: Kendall/Hunt Publishing Company for the World Bank.

WALHI (Wahana Lingkungan Hidup Indonesia). 1991. "Sustainability and Economic Rent in the Forestry Sector." Jakarta. Manuscript.

Wells, Michael, and Katrina Brandon. 1992. *People and Parks*. Washington, D.C.: World Bank.

Wille, Chris. 1990. "Trees on Trial in Central America." *American Forests* (September/October): 21–24, 73.

Wilson, Paul N., and Gary D. Thompson. 1993. "Common Property and Uncertainty: Compensating Coalitions by Mexico's Pastoral *Ejidatarios*." *Economic Development and Cultural Change* 41 (2) (January): 299–318.

World Bank. 1990. *World Development Report 1990.* New York: Oxford University Press for the World Bank.

World Resources Institute. 1992. *World Resources 1992–93.* New York: Oxford University Press.

Zobel, B. J., G. van Wyk, and P. Stahl. 1987. *Growing Exotic Forests.* New York: Wiley Interscience.

Index

About the Author

William Ascher is a professor of public policy studies and political science at Duke University, where he also directs the Sanford Institute of Public Policy. His research covers policy-making processes in developing countries, natural resource policymaking, Latin American political economy, and forecasting methodologies. His books on developing countries include *Scheming for the Poor: The Politics of Redistribution in Latin America* and *Natural Resource Policymaking in Developing Countries* (with Robert G. Healy). As project director of the International Commission for Central American Recovery and Development, he edited *Central American Recovery and Development: The Task Force Studies*. He has also published two books on political-economic forecasting: *Forecasting: An Appraisal for Policymakers and Planners* and *Strategic Planning and Forecasting* (with William Overholt). Professor Ascher is currently writing a book on the political economy of natural resource management that will explore the common elements of policy failures related to the broad range of renewable and nonrenewable resources.